29-12

STE

Please renew/return items by last date shown. Please call the number below:

Renewals and enquiries: 0300 123 4049

Textphone for hearing or
speech impaired users: 0300 123 4041

www.hertfordshire.gov.uk/libraries
L32

Hertfordshire

D1491742

THE 2084 REPORT

THE 2084 REPORT

A HISTORY OF GLOBAL WARMING
FROM THE FUTURE

JAMES LAWRENCE POWELL

HODDER &
STOUGHTON

First published in hardcover in the USA in 2020 by Atria Books
An imprint of Simon & Schuster, Inc.
First published in Great Britain in 2020 by Hodder & Stoughton
An Hachette UK company

1

Interior design by A. Kathryn Barrett

A CIP catalogue record for this title is available from the British Library

Hardback ISBN 978 1 529 31186 0
Trade Paperback ISBN 978 1 529 31182 2
eBook ISBN 978 1 529 31184 6

Printed and bound in Great Britain by Clays Ltd, Elcograf S.p.A.

Hodder & Stoughton policy is to use papers that are natural, renewable
and recyclable products and made from wood grown in sustainable
forests. The logging and manufacturing processes are expected to
conform to the environmental regulations of the country of origin.

Hodder & Stoughton Ltd
Carmelite House
50 Victoria Embankment
London EC4Y 0DZ

www.hodder.co.uk

CONTENTS

THE 2084 REPORT

They say that most writers write for themselves and hope that their book will turn into a best seller. Nowadays, there is no way for any book, no matter how important and well written, to sell enough copies to qualify as a best seller. The big online booksellers depended entirely on the Internet, which, like the rest of our infrastructure, has grown steadily less reliable and less secure and will surely not survive to the end of the century. Almost all the physical bookstores that once could have maintained sales have long been put out of business by the online sellers.

Why then did I write this book, knowing that it will be read mostly by friends and family? Because I am an oral historian. My job is to record significant events in human history using the words of those who experienced them. Thus, we provide the raw material from which other historians can synthesize and generalize. Of course, I also write because I like to, and writing is one pleasure that is still possible. You don't really need a working computer, the Internet, and the so-called Cloud—all you need is pencil and paper.

The master of his approach and my model is the great twentieth-century oral historian Studs Terkel. Two of his books, *"The Good War": An Oral History of World War II*, and *Hard Times: An Oral History of the Great Depression*, captured the effects of those calamities on Americans of all stripes as no other books ever did. All through my career, I have gone back to reread him and he has never failed to inspire me.

Studs traveled to interview people from all walks of life, from the farm to the factory, from city to town, from retirees to youngsters, from the lofty to the man and woman on the street. Like him, most of my subjects are average folks, though I include a few experts and leaders. I wound up interviewing nearly one hundred people, too many for one book, and so I have chosen the interviews that best illustrate what flooding, drought, war, famine, disease, and mass migration of climate refugees have done to humankind.

I feel a special affinity for Studs Terkel because I was born in 2012, exactly one hundred years after his birth. In 1912, global warming was only a theoretical concept. A few scientists thought it might turn out to be real, but they had too little information to regard it as dangerous. Indeed, those scientists understandably thought that a warmer world might be better for humanity. By the year of my birth a century later, it was beyond dispute that global warming was real, caused by humans, and a danger to humanity. Yet thanks to a campaign funded mainly by the giant oil companies of those days, half the public and many politicians chose denial, putting ideology and lies above their grandchildren's future.

I have kept my role to a minimum, showing in italics where I asked a question and otherwise letting my subjects speak for themselves, just as Studs did. For ease of reading, I have grouped chapters by topic, but this is somewhat arbitrary as most regions suffer from more than one effect of global warming. Unless otherwise noted, I used a satellite telephone.

Lexington, Kentucky
December 31, 2084

Today I talk with Robert Madsen III, who, like his father and grandfather before him, is a climate scientist.

Dr. Madsen, I have come to you with a question that people in the second half of this century are compelled to ask.

Those of us alive today are haunted by the question of why, back in the first few decades of this century, before time had run out, people did not act to at least slow global warming. Was it because there was not enough evidence, because scientists could not agree, because there was some better theory to explain the warming that was obviously going on, or something else? Surely our grandparents' generation had a good reason for letting this happen to us—what was it?

Well, I can tell you that this will not be the longest chapter in your book, because the answer is short and simple: They did not have a good reason.

Even at the turn of the century the evidence for man-made global warming was overwhelming, and it only grew stronger until it became undeniable to any rational person—that is, anyone who used reason as their guide. A friend who had trained as a lawyer once asked me whether global warming had been supported by a preponderance of evidence, or beyond reasonable doubt, the higher standard in a criminal case. I answered that global warming had been beyond reasonable doubt, as certain as any scientific theory can be.

If you were to go back to the 2010s and judge the collective opinion of scientists on the basis of what they published in peer-reviewed journals, you would find that by 2020 they were in 100 percent agreement that humans were the cause of global warming. That's not just a round number I plucked out of the air, but the result of a review of nearly twenty thousand peer-reviewed articles from that period.

Hard as it is to conceive, the global warming deniers had no scientific theory of their own to explain the evidence. It would be one thing if people in the tens and twenties had allowed our world to be destroyed because they bet on the wrong theory. But there was no alternative theory. Temperatures rose, wildfires grew worse every year on every continent, sea level went higher and higher, storms got worse, and on and on. Those who denied that humans were responsible had no curiosity about what *was* causing this extreme weather, but they had decided what *was not*: fossil fuels.

All right, that is short and simple. But even deniers without a theory had to have some alternative way to explain the data that convinced scientists. How did they attempt that?

For a while they said that global warming was a hoax, that conspiring scientists had faked the data. Those who deny science always get to the point of claiming conspiracy eventually, for the only other choice is to admit that scientists are right.

If you had been around in those days, how would you have responded to those who claimed that man-made global warming was a conspiracy?

Well, I would have urged people to ask themselves a few simple questions. How was the conspiracy organized? Those twenty thousand articles would have had roughly sixty thousand authors from countries all over the world. How could the hoaxers have kept everything straight? They would have had to use email. But back in the first decade someone stole and published a trove of emails from prominent climate scientists—almost a million words as I recall. Not one word in those emails ever gave any hint of a conspiracy.

Why then did no conspirator ever get caught, write a tell-all memoir, or make a deathbed confession? And why would they have conspired in the first place? In America, the deniers' answer was, "Because they were liberals." But more than half the scientific papers were coming from other countries, where that label did not apply.

But of course, by the 2010s, the deniers did not ask themselves these sorts of questions. To them, that global warming was false was so obvious that the reason scientists would have mounted a hoax no longer mattered.

By the 2020s, lies had come to replace truth not just in regard to science, but in many areas. People preferred to accept a lie that supported their prior belief rather than a truth that undercut that belief. This allowed countries such as Australia, Brazil, Russia, and the United States to elect science deniers to lead them.

Even as late as the early twenties, warming could have been limited to 5.4°F [3°C].[1] But the nations of the world could not bring themselves to even try. By the time they did, even 7.2°F [4°C] was no longer an option. We don't know how high the temperature may go. It's a strange thing: We humans pride ourselves on being ruled by reason, yet with human civilization at stake, we chose ideology and ignorance.

If people thought scientists were so crooked as to fake global warming, it must have been hard to trust scientists on anything else. Did that attitude have an effect on the status of science itself?

My grandfather was a scientist and inspired me to become one too. He told me how, by the late tens, science deniers occupied the White

---

[1] Throughout, I show measurements in both F° and C° and in both metric and U.S. customary units.

House and the top tiers of nearly every government agency. They cut research funding not only for climate science, but for anything having to do with the environment, endangered species, industrial pollution, and so on. The Environmental Protection Agency and the National Science Foundation did not survive the 2020s and overall federal funding for science fell to the level of the 1950s. Grandad said that to him and his colleagues, it almost seemed like "science" had become a dirty word.

Most university scientists back then depended on government grants and had to give up their research programs. Large universities had gotten one-quarter to one-third of their overall funding as overhead on research grants. One of the first things they did was reduce funding for science departments and lay off faculty. Students, seeing no future in studying science, voted with their feet to take classes in other subjects. Science enrollment dwindled, justifying the elimination of more science departments and faculty. Science journals, whose main customers were universities, also fell victim, as the volume of research plummeted and as funding for university libraries dropped and then disappeared. Of course, without research funding and journals, the many science societies also had to close their doors.

In my grandad's book collection, I found a well-thumbed volume titled *The End of History and the Last Man*. We may not be at the End of Science, but you can see it coming.

PART 1
DROUGHT AND FIRE

MOROCCO IN SWITZERLAND

Christiane Mercier is the longtime global-warming correspondent for the French newspaper Le Monde. *In this interview, she speaks to me from several different locations in Europe. Our first conversation in the series took place at the former Swiss ski resort of Zermatt.*

I am making this tour to take stock of what global warming has done to different locations in Europe. I'm standing at the heart of the former Swiss tourism industry, where skiing is no longer possible. Zermatt once had world-class ski slopes and a fabulous view of the Matterhorn. As I look around now, there is no snow to be seen anywhere, not even on the summit of the Matterhorn itself.

To prepare for this interview I did some research on the history of global warming in the Alps. Even fin de siècle, there were ominous signs. In those days the snow line extended down 9,940 feet [3,030 meters], but in the deadly hot summer of 2003, for example, it rose to 15,100 feet [4,600 meters], higher than the summit of the Matterhorn and almost as high as the summit of Mont Blanc, the highest peak west of the Caucasus. The permafrost that held the rock and soil on the Matterhorn melted, sending debris tumbling downhill. You can still see the debris piles resting against, and even inside, the shuttered ski lodges and restaurants.

I could give the same report from Davos, Gstaad, St. Moritz, or any of the once-famous ski resorts in Switzerland, France, and Italy. The Alps have not had permanent snow and ice since the 2040s. I understand that the Rocky Mountain ski slopes have met the same fate.

Meteorologists tell us that the climate of Southern Europe today is the same as it was in Algeria and Morocco when the century began. As measured by temperature and precipitation, Southern Europe is now a desert and the Alps are well on their way to resembling the Atlas Mountains of those days.

Several weeks later Ms. Mercier was in Nerja on Spain's Sun Coast, once host to expatriates and seasonal visitors escaping the cold winters of Germany and the United Kingdom.

Looking south from the waterfront at Nerja, spread before me is the vast, blue Mediterranean. Looking north, stretching seemingly forever is a sea of abandoned buff and ocher condominiums, thousands, tens of thousands—an incomprehensible number, most of them decayed and crumbling. It is not hard to understand why: The countryside is parched and dead. At 2 P.M. in the afternoon in front of the ruins of the Hotel Balcón on the Nerja waterfront, the temperature in the shade is 124°F [51°C], and there is no sea breeze to be felt. I seem to be the only person about, and I do not plan to be about for long.

On the way to Nerja from Córdoba and Granada, I saw the charred remains of tens of thousands of olive trees, the monoculture that used to dominate southern Spain. As the region warmed, olive trees dried out, making them susceptible to fire and disease. Today, olive growing has shifted from Spain and Italy north to France and Germany and even England.

From Nerja, Ms. Mercier traveled to Gibraltar.

I had a great deal of trouble finding transportation to get down here and back. What used to take half a day's drive took me four. Gibraltar used to be one of the British Empire's crown jewels, guarding entrance to and exit from the Mediterranean. But only a few miles away by sea lay Morocco, a proximity that made Gibraltar a natural mecca for climate migrants.

In my research preparing for the trip, I found a report from the 2010s noting that migration to the EU had already risen due to increasing heat and drought and the social disorder that resulted. One study projected that the annual number of migrants would rise from the 350,000 of the tens to twice that by 2100. But this study, like so many from that period regardless of topic, projected the future based on the past and the past was not a good guide when there was a "new normal" every year or two. These projections almost never took into account global warming and its ancillary effects. Now, no one knows how many people have managed to arrive in Europe after fleeing from Africa, the Middle East, and what we used to call Eastern Europe, but certainly the number is in the hundreds of millions, maybe half a billion. And still they come.

By 2050, so many climate refugees had crossed into Gibraltar that England announced it was ceding the territory to the country that had long claimed it. Spain then made a half-hearted effort to govern Gibraltar. But when the desalination plants on which it had depended for water failed, Spain was in no position to replace them. In 2065 it gave up and declared Gibraltar an open city. Since then it has been known by its original name: Jabal Ṭāriq, Mountain of Tariq.

Because of overcrowding and scarce resources, Gibraltar has become a dangerous place. I had to enter disguised as a man and accompanied by armed mercenaries. I did not stay long—but long enough to see that when some said global warming would bring hell and high water, they were not far off.

When next I speak with Ms. Mercier, she has moved up the Mediterranean coast to the Spanish province of Murcia.

From Jabal Ṭāriq I hired a boat to take me northeast to Murcia, stopping at places on the way that my captain said were likely to be safe. If you had visited Murcia in the early years of the century, you would have passed fields full of lettuce and hothouses of ripe tomatoes. You would have seen the new vacation homes and condos springing up everywhere. On the way to the beach, you would have found it hard to avoid passing a green golf course. In such a dry land, where did Spain get the water for all this?

As you know from my reports, before I visit an area, *Je fais mon travail*—I do my homework. I study the history of a city or country so I can understand what I am seeing. Murcia is a case study in how impotent people and governments were to prevent this tragedy of the commons from ruining their lives and their land.

Murcia was always dry, but a lack of rain did not prevent people from behaving as though there would always be plenty of water. If water did not fall from the sky, people found it underground or transferred it from distant snowfields. At the turn of the century, they refused to believe that the day might come when none of these strategies would work.

Until the latter part of the last century, Murcia's farmers grew figs and date palms and, where they had enough water, lemons and other citrus. Then the government arranged to transfer water from less-dry provinces, which allowed the farmers to switch to thirsty crops like lettuce, tomatoes, and strawberries. Developers built as fast as they could, and every new building had to have its own swimming pool. Vacationers needed villas, condos, and enough golf courses so they did not have to wait to tee off. Keeping each of Murcia's golf courses green took hundreds of thousands of gallons of water per day. Someone figured out that to allow a golfer to play one round took 3,000 gallons [11,356 liters] of water. Today, golf has gone the way of hockey and skiing and sports generally.

Had Spanish officials taken global warming seriously and studied Murcia's temperature records, they might have been more cautious. During the twentieth century, Spain warmed twice as much as the Earth overall, and the amount of rainfall declined. Scientists projected that rainfall would drop a further 20 percent by 2020 and 40 percent by 2070. The forecasts turned out to be accurate, though at the time they were made no one had paid any attention. When northern provinces had to cut back their water transfers, Murcia's farmers and towns had to turn to groundwater, causing the water table to drop sharply. A black market in water from illegal wells sprang up, and soon the water table was so deep that pumps could not lift the water to the surface. Scandals were uncovered, with corrupt officials caught taking payoffs in exchange for building permits in areas where there was no water. Unbelievably, gullible people in Britain and Germany continued to buy condos and villas in Spain. They would arrive at their new home or condo, turn on the tap, find that no water emerged, and then look for someone to sue. Then they found out that the fine print on their contract had given the builders and the government an escape clause if an act of God caused a water shortage. Global warming an act of God? *Ne me fais pas rire*; or, as you say, Don't make me laugh.

As the water dried up, farmers switched back to figs and date palms. But as the century went on and the scientists' forecasts proved correct or, more often, conservative, even those desert crops could not be grown economically in Spain. By the 2050s, agriculture in Murcia had essentially ended and the vacation homes and condos stood empty. Today, except for its derelict buildings, Murcia is indistinguishable from the North African desert of a century ago.

When next I talk with Ms. Mercier, she has reached her home in Paris.

On the way home, I passed through the Loire Valley, a region that used to produce some of the most outstanding wines in the world: Chinon, Muscadet, Pouilly-Fumé, Sancerre, Vouvray, and others. All are gone. The problem was that as temperatures rise, grapes mature earlier, raising their sugar content and lowering their acidity. Such grapes produce a coarser wine with a higher alcohol content. If temperatures had only risen a degree or two—had we stayed below the *point de rupture* of carbon dioxide levels—then, though Vouvray might not have tasted the same, it still would have been drinkable. Possibly an expert might even have recognized it as some variation on Vouvray. But the temperature has gone up by 9°F [5° C]. Wine grapes will not grow in the Loire Valley now and the industry here, as in the rest of France, is defunct. If you want wine today, go to the former UK or Scandinavia.

Right now I am standing in the shade of the Arc de Triomphe at midafternoon on July 1, 2084. It is a good thing I am in the shade, because the temperature is 115°F [46°C]. To stand in direct sunlight in this heat for more than a few minutes is to guarantee heatstroke. Looking around, I see only a handful of vehicles moving. Few people are on the street. Even at night it is too hot to sit outdoors, as the heat absorbed during the day by the steel and concrete of Paris is released. The City of Light has become, like so many, the City of Heat, and her sidewalk cafés are just a memory.

From Paris our reporter travels to Calais on the English Channel.

On the way here, travel was so difficult that I almost gave up and returned to Paris. Before long no one will be able to make a trip like this safely. Just as Gibraltar was the natural entry point to Europe for Africans trying to move north to escape the killing heat, so Calais, only 20 miles [32 km] across the channel from Dover, has been the natural exit point for those trying to reach the cooler climes of the former United Kingdom. In the 2020s, many Britons wanted to reduce both legal and illegal immigration. For a while they got their wish, but by the late 2030s, the number of illegal immigrants arriving in the former UK began to rise and has kept on rising. Calais's main function now is to serve that illegal migration. Just as I saw few Spaniards in southern Spain, most of the people I see and talk with in Calais are not French or British, but Arabs, Africans, Syrians, and Slavs. The only thing they have in common appears to be that they come from elsewhere and are determined to reach the White Cliffs of Dover. Some migrants try to swim the Channel, but few survive it. The tumult here reminds me of a scene I remember from old newsreels showing the chaos at the Fall of Paris as the Germans approached and Parisians scattered to the winds.

At the port of Calais, I see a reenactment of another scene from World War II: the escape of the British Expeditionary Force from Dunkirk in hundreds of watercraft of every description. Now the water is filled with another mélange of vessels, crowded to their railings with people headed for the promised land of England, where the smuggling operators wait to receive them—or so they hope.

I had thought I would get passage on one of those vessels and report from England, but I am utterly defeated and depressed at what I have seen. *Je me rends.*

PHOENIX DESCENDING

Born and raised in Phoenix, Steve Thompson is a seventy-two-year-old hydraulic engineer who once worked for the Central Arizona Project. He moved to Saskatchewan and became a Canadian citizen before the Canadian-American War.

Steve, when did your family come to Arizona?

My great-grandparents moved to Phoenix just after World War II, at the same time as a lot of other ex–service member families, all following the American dream. And by and large they found it.

All through the second half of the last century and for a time in this one, the demand for housing in Phoenix kept the real estate boom going, and that kept everything else booming. People enjoyed the good life and forgot they were living in a desert that had only 8 inches [200 mm] of rainfall each year.

Most people really had no idea where the water that flowed from their taps came from. They may have known that there was something called the Central Arizona Project, which brought water from Lake Mead on the lower Colorado River into Phoenix. But where did the Colorado River get its water? From melting snowfields on the western slopes of the Rockies many hundreds of miles away. If something happened to change the amount of snow that fell in the Rockies or the timing of the melt season, Phoenix could be in real trouble. But no one worried about that. At the turn of the century, those in charge of planning for central Arizona thought that the population would rise to nearly 7 million people by 2050. In hindsight, that was a ridiculous assumption. When my great-grandparents moved here in 1950, Phoenix proper had only about 100,000 people. The year I was born, 2012, it had 1.6 million. Now it's back down, headed toward 100,000 again. And even that may be too many.

Until the 2020s, everything just seemed to get better in Phoenix. Sure, through the tens it got hotter each year, but all our buildings were air-conditioned, so we just stayed indoors during the middle of the summer days. We never really thought about how we would get by if there were power shortages that kept us from turning on our air conditioners whenever we felt like it. We didn't adequately consider that if the Colorado ran low, which climate scientists forecast it would under global warming, then there would be less water turning the turbines in Hoover and Glen Canyon Dams and less electrical power. Thus, if we had a bad-enough drought, we would also have a power shortage.

When did you realize that things had changed?

I think I can pin it down to the hour, to the most vivid memory of my life. I was fifteen years old, so it must have been 2027. It was a hot summer morning and my mother answered a knock at the door to find two men standing there, both in uniform. One had a Smith & Wesson .38 special strapped to his hip; the other carried a toolbox. That pistol made a big impression on me. Both men wore the badges of the city water department. As part of a citywide program, they had come to install a remote-control valve that would limit how much water my family could use in a twenty-four-hour period: 75 gallons [284 liters] per person. When we reached that limit, the valve would automatically close and we would get no more water until 12:01 A.M. the next day. Of course, the water department and the newspapers and TV had warned that rationing was coming, but the full impact of it did not hit our family until those two men showed up at our door.

If the citywide ration of 75 gallons per person per day turned out not to save enough water, the city could remotely reprogram the valves for a lower limit. Anyone could see that was bound to happen. The penalty for tampering with the shutoff valves was a fine and a reduced ration. A repeat offense would earn the homeowner a mandatory two years in jail with no time off for good behavior. In case anyone failed to get the message, electronic billboards around the city posted videos of the latest water cheats undergoing a public "perp walk."

Having to get by on 75 gallons and then less as the city lowered the ration, when only two decades earlier the average Phoenix resident had consumed well over 200 gallons [757 liters] per day, meant we had to change the way we lived. Families had to prepare water budgets just as they prepared financial ones, but there was a big difference. Back then, a family could still borrow money or charge purchases to a credit card, but no one in Phoenix was going to loan you water or sell it even for cash on the barrelhead.

We retrofitted our homes with low-flush toilets, faucets that ran for only a few seconds, and bathtubs. Forget taking a shower—no one did that anymore and anyway having a showerhead in your home was illegal. Instead we took a tub bath once a week, the way they used to do in the pioneer days, and used gray water for flushing our toilets. Some of us saved even more water by using chamber pots or installing outdoor privies.

The authorities outlawed watering lawns and soon there were none. The scores of golf courses all around Phoenix closed. To have a patch of green on your property back then was to invite a visit from the water police. As more people abandoned their homes, lawns simply dried up and blew away on the wind.

The trouble was, these conservation measures did not work. Sure, per capita consumption went down, but even into the 2030s, people just kept moving here in spite of the warning signs that there was not going to be enough water or power. There always seems to be a gap between people's perception and reality. If you cut average consumption by half, but double the population, you are right back where you started. Since you can't force people to move, all you can do is ration water and then lower the ration.

To be outdoors in midday was to take your life in your hands. Though I was gone by then, in the 2040s Phoenix was as hot and sometimes hotter than Death Valley had been in 2000. All you could do was stay indoors and, when you had to go out, run for the next air-conditioned refuge. But air-conditioning required electrical power and the water shortage caused the hydrodams to produce less, and pretty soon the city began to ration electricity as well. You could no longer count on finding one of those air-conditioned refuges. In midday, the streets and sidewalks of Phoenix became virtually empty. You never saw children or pets outside anymore. The elderly had their own problems. For them, air-conditioning was a matter of life and death, and those who could not afford it or had no way to leave gave Phoenix the highest senior death rate of any city in the country.

Just about every aspect of life in central Arizona had changed for the worse. The time was long past when anyone could cling to the illusion that the heat and drought were part of some natural cycle that we Arizonans could outwait. Bad as things were, they were going to get worse and stay that way for as far ahead as anyone could see. For Americans, especially those in the Southwest, home to the American dream, that was a new concept.

I watched my parents age prematurely as they realized that their senior years were not going to be the pleasant time for which they had planned and saved. Anyone could see that the intelligent thing to do was to get out of Arizona, but with thousands of new homes standing empty in half-finished, waterless subdivisions, home prices had plummeted. Since my parents could not recover the equity in our home, they did not have the capital or credit to buy a new one in some cooler, wetter climate, where, in any case, demand had driven home prices out of reach. Younger couples willing to take their chances often just walked away from their homes and mortgages, not even bothering to lock the doors, for they knew they would never be back. But for the elderly, leaving was not an option. For me it was, and in 2032, I bid my parents and Phoenix a sad goodbye and headed for Canada.

Marta Soares is a Brazilian anthropologist and the last director of Fundação Nacional do Índio (FUNAI), the National Indian Foundation, whose mission had been to protect Indian interests and culture. With Ms. Soares is Megaron Txcucarramae, an indigenous native of Brazil and the last surviving member of the Metyktire tribe, one of the branches of the Kayapo people. I first interview Megaron with Ms. Soares translating, then I interview Ms. Soares directly.

Ms. Soares, please introduce your friend.

Though we are talking on the telephone, you should know that Megaron Txcucarramae is wearing the characteristic Kayapo headdress—*cabeça-vestido*, we say in Portuguese—made from the feathers of the scarlet macaw and the green oropendola. Megaron wished to wear this family heirloom in honor of the interview, saying it would put him in the mood to tell you of the sad history of his people. His life spans the destruction of the Amazon rain forest and the tragic end of a way of life that existed for thousands of years before the white man. In the lifetime of this one person, the Amazon has turned from a Garden of Eden into a bed of ashes, and Megaron has been witness to the destruction.

I have spent much time with Megaron and his people. I will translate your questions into his language and his responses back to you in English.

Megaron: I am an old man now and my days are numbered. They tell me that I am the last living member of the Metyktire tribe and I believe them, for I have not met another Metyktire in many years. I have outlived my children and even my grandchildren. They died from the white man's diseases and some, I think, from giving up hope. Yet there is something worse than outliving your own blood, and that is to outlive every member of your tribe and even the forest that has been your home since ancient times.

Once we forest people were as many as the birds. Now even the days of the Kayapo are few. The green forest that nourished our people since the beginning of time is almost gone and soon we will be gone too. We do not recognize this world, and I for one do not care to live in it much longer.

I was born in the year 1994 by your calendar and never saw a white man until I was thirteen years old. We Metyktire had decided many years ago to avoid contact with whites, because our shamans foretold that they would bring evil upon us. We broke off from the Kayapo and retreated deep into the forest. Except for a few chance meetings, we never saw another man or woman other than our own tribe members. But by your year 2007, there were only eighty-seven of us left. Many were old and some were sick. Our elders could see that soon the Metyktire would be few, that fire, disease, storm, or drought could easily wipe us out. They decided we had no choice but to come out of our jungle hideout and rejoin the Kayapo. We sent two of our men to meet with them and they greeted us like long-lost brothers. We were terrified that we would have to meet large numbers of white people, whom we had only heard about, but the Kayapo protected us and allowed only a small team of doctors and nurses to examine us. They were afraid that, having been out of contact with any other society for so many decades, we might get some of your white man's diseases. Some of us did get sick, but no one died. Now I am used to white skin, but back then it was a terrible shock.

When did you begin to notice changes in the rain forest around you?

I remember it was in the summer when I turned eleven. For many years our tribe had smelled the smoke from fires, some set by lightning, but many lit by settlers burning the forest so they could plant crops or raise cattle on the land. Every year there seemed to be more smoke and the fires came closer. But that summer (Soares: It was 2005 by your calendar) the entire sky turned black and stayed that way for months. It was hard to breathe, and we coughed constantly. The sun could only poke through now and then. The smoke made it seem like the prophecies of our shamans were coming true. We asked ourselves, could all the forest burn? We did not know, but it did not seem impossible anymore. Even though the fires did not come onto our territory, we knew that they might one day. If they did, we would have no way to escape and there would be no other people to help us.

As the shamans had prophesied, the big fires were just the start of our troubles. Each year a little less rain fell, it got a little hotter, more of the forest burned, and fewer trees grew to take the place of those that burned. There was not enough water to grow crops, and those that did get started often withered and died. The rivers began to dry up and many became too shallow for boats. At first, we would see a few dead fish floating on the surface, then as the river shrank, we saw more and more until sometimes the entire surface would be covered from bank to bank with the bodies of dead fish. Then the rivers kept shrinking until there was no water left for our canoes, and in the river channels grass grew. Where we had floated for generations, now we could walk.

I have heard some of the educated Kayapo talk about why it happened, but I do not understand it. How could what people do in lands far away cause our forests to burn? They say it is something in the air that you cannot see or smell, some poison that makes it get hotter and drives the rain away. I have asked Marta many times how that could be, and she has patiently explained it, but I must be too old to understand. What I do know from my own eyes and from talking with her and Kayapo who have traveled far is that almost all the forest has burned, taking most of the native people with it. The Metyktire, the Kayapo, the Yanomami—we are all nearly gone now. But what I would like to find out before I die is what made our forest burn.

Megaron, let me ask your friend Marta to answer your question. Ms. Soares, who burned the Amazon?

Soares: I have to confess that, though I understand the answer, I still find it hard to accept that any power on Earth has caused the loss of almost all the Amazon rain forest in less than a century. Megaron will tell you that people had always known that the Amazon forest could burn—they had been burning it on purpose since he was a boy. He wants to know why they did not stop the fires from getting out of control. Didn't they care? We Portuguese speakers have a saying, "*dançar à beira do caos*"—to dance on the edge of chaos. That is what the world did back then, but we danced too close.

We can explain the science of global warming and how it led the rain forest to burn, but for me, at least, that only makes the answer more painful and the outcome less excusable. We know that Man burned the rain forest, that it was not an act of God. It was preventable. How could those who were supposed to lead and protect nations, and who had ample warning, allow the Amazon and its indigenous tribes to disappear? Many of those tribes had chosen not to try to survive in our world, then we destroyed the only world they could survive in.

Amazonians had always practiced slash-and-burn agriculture,

but, in the second half of the twentieth century, nonnative farmers and settlers began to use the method. Between 1970 and the turn of the century, more than 232,000 square miles [600,900 sq km] of Amazon rain forest burned. Between May 2000 and August 2006, Brazil lost nearly 58,000 square miles [150,220 sq km] of forest—an area larger than Greece. By the second decade of this century, farmers had deliberately burned nearly 25 percent of the entire Amazon forest, and, in spite of the efforts of conservationists, more was being lost each year. Around the world, even when we knew that global warming was happening and was dangerous, and that trees could absorb some of the deadly carbon dioxide, the world destroyed 30 million acres of rain forest each year. So you see, even without global warming, in time we probably would have burned the entire Amazon forest. We seemed powerless to act not only in the interest of native peoples but in our own. Now we know how much we needed that rain forest.

I was an anthropologist, not a climate scientist, but I have learned from colleagues that a rain forest is vulnerable in several ways. As long as a dense forest canopy 90 to 135 feet high [27 to 41 meters] provides shade, the debris on the forest floor can remain moist, so that it rarely burns. But when one part of the forest burns, more sunlight reaches the floor of the burned area and the perimeter around it. That dries out the dead leaves and branches and other debris. Grasses, bamboo, and other flammable plants colonize the area and increase the amount of combustible fuel, making it more likely that the area will burn again, this time more intensely, for longer, and over a larger area. Thus, when you burn part of the forest, you make other fires more likely—a feedback, they call it. Also, when part of the forest burns, there is less water vapor and more smoke in the atmosphere above, both of which cause less rain to fall, which leads more of the forest to dry and burn. These vicious cycles are enough to make a person believe that there really is a *satanás*—a devil.

Scientists at the turn of the century had forecast that by 2100 the Amazon basin would warm between 9 and 14.5°F [5 and 8°C] and that rainfall would drop by 20 percent. But the Amazon climate warmed and dried even faster. By 2030, 60 percent of the rain forest was gone. By 2050, 80 percent, and today, 95 percent. Within another decade or two, all of the Amazon rain forest except for scattered patches will have burned, spelling the end for all the indigenous peoples and thousands of species. The Amazon was once home to one out of every four or five mammal, fish, bird, and tree species. Now many of them are gone, taking whole ecosystems with them. The Maranhão babaçu forests, the Marañón dry forests, the cloud forests of Bolivia and all their species are gone, never to return.

Before it burned, the Amazon was so vast and green that it helped control the climate of the entire planet. The forest was a huge heat sponge, keeping hundreds of billions of tons of carbon dioxide out of the atmosphere. They say that the Amazon rain forest evaporated 8 trillion metric tons of water each year. That water was critical to the formation of cumulus clouds, which released the rain that sustained the forest. I cannot remember when I last saw one of those clouds. What we see instead is smoke. The Amazon was so critical to the world's climate that scientists believe its loss has caused less rain to fall in Central America, in the midwestern United States, and even as far away as India.

The Amazon held a vast amount of carbon that deforestation and burning have now released back into the atmosphere. According to one estimate, the loss of the Amazon rain forest has raised the total amount of carbon in the atmosphere by 140 billion tons, equivalent to about fifteen years' worth of annual global emissions in the year 2000.

So, back to Megaron's question. Who burned the Amazon?

We have another saying, *"Uma boa pergunta é a metade da resposta"*—a good question is half the answer. The people who could have prevented global warming but stood by and let it happen, not only the so-called leaders but also the people who elected them—they burned the Amazon. My people and your people, not Megaron's.

Australia was one of the first countries to feel the effects of global warming and one of the first to take action. Dr. Evonne Emerson held the Kevin Rudd Chair of Australian History at Australian National University until it closed in 2055. I called her at her home in Perth.

Dr. Emerson, you have deep roots in Australia.

Yes, our family records show that ten generations ago, in 1855, my ancestors arrived from England and got off the boat at Portland. They began to prospect in the goldfields of Victoria. Our family never found much gold, but they did find a good life here in Australia.

But global warming was a particular threat to your country, wasn't it?

Remember that Australia is a continent, an island, and a country—all three. Other continents have their deserts and drought, but Australia had more of both. We are the driest continent outside Antarctica, with the lowest rainfall and the lowest average river discharge by a wide margin. If you had looked at a map of our climate zones back at the turn of the century, you would have seen that half of Australia was effectively desert and another quarter was grasslands. Today, the grasslands have nearly disappeared as the deserts have taken over. Only along the coast, especially in New South Wales, did Australia have enough rainfall back then to amount to anything. We could not afford to lose a drop.

That said, my reading of history is that Australia's familiarity with drought turned out to be a benefit. We did not have to imagine what a severe drought would do; more than one had already done it.

Drought is so important in Australia's history that several clauses in our constitution refer to it. Indeed, were it not for drought, Australia's states might be a set of small, independent countries like Europe instead of a federation like America. I say that because in the 1890s, a terrible drought killed half of Australia's sheep and cattle, causing a severe recession. That drought was the proximate reason the six colonies banded together in a commonwealth. Not surprisingly for such a dry land, the negotiations nearly broke down over the amount of water each state would receive. The fundamental problem was that for most of its length, our River Murray forms the border between New South Wales and Victoria and supplies the water to four of Australia's six states. As in the eternal water battles between your states of California and Arizona, each thought it deserved the lion's share of the water. I suppose those who thought that a river makes an ideal boundary between states had not reckoned with the river running dry.

In 1915 Australia adopted the River Murray Waters Agreement, in which those states upstream guaranteed minimum flows downstream with the remainder divided equally. That in turn started a binge of construction: dams, weirs, locks, and other waterworks that left the Murray and its main tributary, the Darling, little more than a plumbing system.

By the end of the twentieth century, the Murray–Darling was providing the great majority of Australia's irrigation water. With so much of our agriculture depending on irrigation, we had to suck every drop from the Murray–Darling and indeed, we sucked it dry. By 2000 we had consumed over three-fourths of the river's flow, so much that its mouth began to silt up. The lower Murray became dangerously salty and nonnative carp drove out the native fish, exterminating several species. The river became so threatened that Australian officials scrapped the old compact and replaced it with a new agreement. It contained some radical provisions that promised to save the river, if anything could: Irrigators would no longer receive federal subsidies and would have to pay more, discouraging them from using river water. Farmers, not taxpayers, would pay to maintain the river's infrastructure. Use of water to preserve the environment would receive equal priority with commercial uses. Farmers and irrigators could trade water both within states and between them. The agreement put Australia ahead of most countries in water management, but in hindsight it proved too little too late.

When did you realize that all your efforts might not be enough?

There were two events in 2028 that really shocked us. One concerned our signature athletic event, the Australian Open tennis tournament, which brought Australia and our then beautiful city of Melbourne to the world stage. The temperature had been rising at the event throughout the 2010s, even while our Aussie leaders were denying global warming. In late 2019, the worst wildfires in the history of a country of fire broke out and burned an area nearly five times the size of Switzerland, if you can believe that. Did that change the tune of the deniers? No, they just sang louder.

Then, in 2020, several matches had to be suspended because of high temperature and the pall of smoke from those fires. Over the next few years, players used ice packs during court changes and each year more matches had to be delayed or played at night. The trouble was, a hard-surface tennis court soaks up heat during the day and gives it off at night, so moving to nighttime matches did not help much. Some top players began to boycott the tournament. Then, in 2028, during the mixed doubles final, two players died from heatstroke, right in front of thousands of people in the stands and millions watching at home. That was the last Australian Open match ever played. Also that

year, the lower 600 miles [966 km] of the River Murray went completely dry. Losing both the Open and the Murray really shocked us.

Our Commonwealth Scientific and Industrial Research Organi-
sation (CSIRO) had given us ample warning that global warming was
real and dangerous. They told us that Australia had the highest greenhouse gas emissions per capita of any country. Also, that during the
second half of the twentieth century, average temperatures in Australia
had risen by 1.6°F [0.9°C], more than the average *global* temperature
had risen during *all* of the twentieth century. Australia was not only the
driest continent, but it may have become the hottest. In the same half
century, both the number of extreme hot days and average nighttime
temperatures rose. Australia's nighttime temperatures were particularly
telling, because no denier could claim, as they did in the United States
and elsewhere, that urban heat islands had caused the nighttime rise—
Australia had only a few, widely scattered cities. To make matters worse,
average rainfall in the Murray–Darling Basin decreased between 1950
and 2000. But the CSIRO told us that worse was to come. It's estimated
that the flow of the Murray–Darling system would drop by 5 percent in
twenty years and 15 percent in fifty years. But the worst-case scenario
would raise these to 20 percent less water in twenty years and 50 percent
in fifty years. As we know today, the worst case turned out to be reality.

Even though Australia was one of the first developed countries
to take serious action to adapt to global warming, it still took longer
for us to get started than it should have. One reason for the delay was
that Australia had the most organized and powerful carbon lobby of
any nation. This Greenhouse Mafia, as they were nicknamed, lobbied
on behalf of Australia's coal, auto, oil, and aluminum industries to prevent legislation that would cost their companies money. During the
Howard administration, these polluters gained such access that they
actually drafted bills and regulations that became law or policy with

little or no revisions. Something similar happened when your president Donald Trump put former fossil fuel lobbyists in charge of key government agencies. But like America, we continued to vote in climate deniers who refused to believe the evidence of their eyes.

How did the Aussie national character play into your response to global warming?

Our history and character were important—that is the reason I gave you the little history lesson when we began talking. If our ancestors had not been hardy, stubborn folk, they would never have made it Down Under in the first place and when they got here would soon have given up. To colonize the driest continent, the first rule had to be "don't panic." Droughts would come, yes, but grit your teeth and bear it and they would eventually end. By the beginning of this century, every mature Australian had lived through at least one drought, each of which had eventually broken. Thus, the strategy that had served us was to hunker down, husband your water, and wait it out. If you were a stockman, some or most of your animals might die, but enough would survive so that when the rain returned, you could rebuild your herd.

One of the worst droughts in Australia's long history of drought struck in the late 1990s. Dredgers at the mouth of the Murray had to work round the clock to keep it from silting in completely. We substantially cut water supplies to irrigators and the city of Adelaide. Our rice crop crashed, causing many farmers to switch to wine grapes, but the wine industry only lasted to the 2030s. People can live without Riesling but not without rice.

Even though 2008 saw some good La Niña rain, the drought had so depleted the reservoirs and left the ground so parched that the rain did not make much difference. Sydney was going through one of its worst droughts ever; by 2005, its reservoirs were severely depleted.

Over on the west coast, Perth's water supply was at an all-time low, causing the city to build desalination plants. Our scientists and the new Rudd government told us that these conditions were apt to become permanent and that we had to act, but we chose to ignore them and elect a succession of science-denying prime ministers. But by the mid 2020s we had come to our senses and decided to face facts and take the bit in our mouths like true blue Aussies.

How did the desalination plants work out for Australia?

Indeed, one of our first moves early in the century had been to build desalting plants in Adelaide, Perth, and Sydney. The plants were not supposed to produce all the water that each city would need, but enough to make a difference. The plant at Perth, for example, when running at full capacity supplied about 17 percent of the city's water needs at the turn of the century. But as Perthians conserved water, the fraction supplied by desalting rose. In 2000, per capita water consumption in Perth was about 130 gallons [492 liters] per day. Simply restricting to two days per week the use of sprinklers for watering lawns and gardens brought consumption down to 110 gallons [416 liters] per day. In the late '20s Perth banned the use of sprinklers and closed its golf courses. Sure, the golfers complained, but by then it was even hotter and drier, and their cries of woe got them a right laugh, that's for sure. We went to full reuse of gray water—drainage from showers and laundry—which amounted to about 30 percent of Perth's household consumption. Perth prohibited new grass lawns and began a "cash for grass" program to pay existing homeowners to remove their lawns and replace them using xeriscaping, cactus, stones, or whatever they liked—as long as it looked good and did not need water. Showers were banned and homeowners were subsidized so they could retrofit existing homes. We raised the price of municipal water to the point where it hurt and adopted a tiered pricing system so that the more water used, the higher the rate. Early in the century farmers paid less than one-tenth as much for water as did municipal users. Most cities found they could not get away with raising the price to irrigators until they had completely eliminated water for lawns and gardens. Once that happened, the price to farmers began to rise sharply and the amount they used dropped. Of course, we had to keep some farm production, so we tweaked the price of irrigation water continually so as not to drive farmers out of business.

Perth was prepared to place automatic shut-off valves on residential water lines, but it never came to that. By 2030, per capita water consumption had fallen to 50 gallons [189 liters] per day, which meant that the desalting plant could supply almost half of Perth's total water consumption. Desalting plants need a lot of energy, but the Perth plant got its power from a wind farm. So, unlike most other desalting plants, the Perth desalter did not cost much to operate and did not add to greenhouse gas emissions. But ultimately, in Australia as elsewhere, desalination could help but could not solve the problem.

We also tried to cut our CO_2 emissions. In the early years of the century, we had no auto mileage requirement. By 2030, we had introduced a requirement of 80 miles per gallon. Even though the auto industry had whined that it would not be able to produce cars with such high fuel efficiency at a profit, in fact they did, and people flocked to buy them. Today, of course, the few cars on the road are electric, powered by solar panels. To find a gasoline-powered car, you have to go to a museum, if you can find one open. But the most insidious thing about global warming was that one country by itself could make little difference. It took all countries acting together, but they did not. In the 2020s, as we were getting tougher and trying everything we could think of to reduce emissions, the Japanese, frightened by the Fukushima nuclear accident, built twenty-two new coal plants!

We did recognize early that if the population of Australia were to grow, the extra people would simply consume more of everything, when in fact we would have less of everything except heat. So, an increase of, say, 10 percent in population would mean a decline of 10 percent in our standard of living. To prevent that, we restricted immigration to New Zealanders, students, skilled migrants, and temporary workers. If you did not belong to one of those groups, you could not enter Australia except for a brief visit. We beefed up our immigration department to enforce those rules.

Although the fertility rate necessary for a stable population is about 2.1 children per woman, early in the century Australia's rate was only 1.76. That meant we did not have to implement population controls as did many countries. Just to be on the safe side, we established a massive education program showing what would happen if Australia's population rose as much in the next fifty years as it had in the last fifty and asked each family to do its part. We provided every form of contraception at no cost. We made abortions safe, easy to get, and free, no questions asked. The result was that Australia's population declined from 22 million in 2010 to 18 million in 2050. That reduction had the same effect per capita as if we had increased resources by roughly 20 percent.

Few countries adapted to global warming as well as Australia and we are proud of that. We knew drought as few did and we used that knowledge to our advantage. But we had another advantage: our isolation. As the world has learned the hard way, the countries that adapted best to global warming typically became meccas for climate refugees. If Australia had had neighbors across a border like yours with Mexico, or even across an easily navigable sea like the Strait of Gibraltar, no doubt the climate refugees would have overrun us too. But they had no way to get here except by boat. A few did set out in makeshift boats from the Philippines and Indonesia, but our coast guard soon picked them up.

On the other hand, our isolation and the collapse of international travel destroyed our tourist income. The Great Barrier Reef alone used to bring in almost seven billion dollars annually—but who wants to come to see its skeleton? Who wants to stare at Ayers Rock in the middle of nowhere? Anyone who wants to view desolation probably does not need to leave home.

Still, on balance I think our isolation helped Australia. It is strange to think that Australia's location in the antipodes, which was the reason the British sent our prisoner ancestors Down Under in the first place, turned out to be our salvation.

What does the future hold for Australia?

No one can know, can they? Our isolation has certainly put our fate in our own hands. With international trade and shipping having broken down, whatever we need we have to grow or make ourselves. It pains me to say this, but a country so dry with no way to import produce cannot feed as many people as now live in Australia. Our agronomists estimate that by abandoning most of the west and the interior and concentrating people in areas that still have enough rain and are not unbearably hot, Australia could sustain a population of about 10 million. Assuming, that is, global warming doesn't just get steadily worse. Then all bets are off here and everywhere.

Dr. Emerson, if decades ago people had been able to foresee the future and understand what has happened to Australia, what do you think the lesson would have been?

That question makes me think of my grandfather. When he was a young man, he loved to read science fiction from the post–World War II years.

Particularly a genre called postapocalyptic fiction, in which authors imagined the world after a global nuclear war. When I was a teenager, I found many of those books in his library and read them. Some had immense power—I remember *Earth Abides, A Canticle for Leibowitz*, and especially *On the Beach*, by the famous author Nevil Shute. These books made readers understand the true danger of nuclear war and no doubt helped to prevent one. None had more impact than *On the Beach*. It was set after a Northern Hemisphere nuclear war but before the deadly fallout had reached Australia. Yet it was coming, and everyone knew it, giving a powerful sense of impending doom to Australians and to an American submarine crew stationed in Australia.

On the Beach brought home to people everywhere the lesson that no corner of the Earth, no matter how distant and isolated, could escape the effects of global nuclear war. The same is true today of a global disaster that no one in Shute's day could imagine. Australia is as well positioned as any country to avoid the worst of global warming. Yet though it may take longer, its effects are nevertheless going to reach here—not if, but when. For people everywhere, there is no haven safe from global warming. The atmosphere, which Shute imagined carrying the deadly atomic fallout and which now carries excessive CO_2, reaches everywhere. That would have been the lesson for our grandparents' generation: If you let global warming happen, no country will escape.

Professor Patrick Thornton is retired from the University of California at Santa Barbara. His academic specialty was the role of man-made global warming on wildfires, which, sad to say, brought his laboratory right to his front door.

Professor Thornton, tell me how your family came to settle in Santa Barbara.

We were Kiwis originally. My grandfather was the first; he came over in the 1960s. He eventually became professor of geology at UCSB. His son, my father, did likewise, so I had it in my blood and became the third generation to teach there. Santa Barbara is where our roots came to be and a great place it was, with the university one of the best in the world and the Mediterranean climate unexcelled anywhere. You could say that Santa Barbara still has a Mediterranean climate, because both places are 8°F [4.4°C] hotter than they were when my grandfather and grandmother arrived. Or you could say there is no such thing as a Mediterranean climate anymore.

Sadly, UCSB is a pale shadow of what it was in its heyday, the tax base that supported the UC system having shrunk more than anyone could have imagined when I was born in 2005. The university writ large was one of the great human inventions, but all are now suffering, and many have closed. By the end of this century, more will have shut their doors and sometime in the next one, the last university will be gone. We could well ask why, if universities were so successful at educating people, their millions of alumni did not rise up to stop man-made global warming.

One of the hardest things about being an academic and a climate scientist in this century is not just the decline in funding for higher education. No, what really hurt was that the public and the politicians, the very people who had handed our country over to the climate deniers and whose support we needed, turned against the educated class in general and against scientists in particular. We became the villains, the victims who got blamed. But unlike the majority of people, when my children ask me what I did to try to stop man-made global warming, I have an answer. My scientist colleagues and I tried but failed. Better that than not to have tried at all.

How did global warming affect your hometown of Santa Barbara?

The city lies between the Santa Barbara Channel to the south, and only a few miles to the north, the Santa Ynez Mountains. I remember a friend who surfed in the morning, and, just to show he could do it, got in his car and drove to the mountains and skied in the afternoon. The business district was near the coast and residences were inland, so that the rising mountainside gave many Santa Barbara homeowners a wonderful view out over the city and on to the Channel Islands. It's rare to see them now because of the smoke from wildfires, although that has started to wane as there is less acreage left to burn.

As this deadly century wore on, what had been a major attraction turned into a threat. The mountains and the beach began to seem like the jaws of a vise that would squeeze the life out of Santa Barbara, forcing the city to fight a war on two fronts, usually a losing proposition. Let me start with the sea and then talk about fire.

In 2012, Santa Barbara city commissioned a report assessing its vulnerability to sea level rise by the end of the twenty-first century. The report predicted that the sea might have risen by 6.5 feet [2 meters], the high end of such projections and one that climate deniers derided. But the projection turned out to be accurate.

The California coast is different from the Atlantic Seaboard, where it is mostly beach from New Jersey to Key West. Here we have our beaches, but also sea cliffs and even mountains facing the waves, as at Big Sur. Thus, we had to not only worry about losing our beaches to a rise in sea level but also about the higher seas and stronger storms triggering more erosion, undercutting the sea cliffs, and causing them to retreat and any houses built on them to collapse. Sea-cliff erosion had always been a problem in Santa Barbara, but this century has seen it get dramatically worse. In most of the world, living on high land was a protection against flooding, but if your home was on a coastal sea cliff, you had a worse problem to worry about.

The 2012 report covered the danger from cliff erosion and flooding, projecting each ahead to 2050 and 2100. It is sad to go back and read that report now, as I did to prepare for our interview, and see what an accurate warning it gave and how sound its recommendations were. I'm sure I am not the only person you've interviewed who has come to wonder whether there is something about our species that makes us unable to act no matter how clear the warning, when the forecast danger lies decades in the future. The fatal flaw of *Homo sapiens* may be that we don't do anything until we absolutely have to, and by then it is often too late.

Some parts of the university campus and nearby Isla Vista, where many students lived, were built atop sea cliffs. Even in my grandfather's day, a section of the cliff would collapse and take the houses above with it. But since then, sea level, wave height, and storm frequency have all increased, accelerating the rate of erosion. The report projected that the retreat of the cliffs could reach 160 feet [49 meters] by 2100, but it has already reached 200 feet [61 meters]. Much of IV has become unlivable and several campus buildings near the cliffs have collapsed.

One desirable Santa Barbara neighborhood was the Mesa, near

downtown and Santa Barbara City College. Many homes there were within 50 feet [15 meters] of the cliffs. The Mesa cliff edge was projected to retreat by 525 feet [160 meters] by 2100, which looks to be accurate, making the district uninhabitable.

The report also looked at flooding and the effect of the hundred-year storm, which comes about every twenty-five years now, riding atop 5 feet [1.5 meters] of sea level rise. It accurately forecast that the Santa Barbara Airport, parts of the City College campus, and the lowest section of the city to the east of downtown, inland fifteen blocks from the shore, would flood every few years. They have, taking out the desalination and waste treatment plants, the bird refuge, and Stearns Wharf in the process.

What about the threat from the other direction, from the mountains?

The particular arrangement of land and sea at Santa Barbara and its location on the California coast subject it to two different kinds of dangerous winds that can fan fires. The sundowners brew up due to differences in air pressure between the mountains and the sea below. They rush down the slopes from the crest of the Santa Ynez Mountains toward the ocean. As the air descends, it heats, dries, and flows faster, making the resulting fires impossible to defend. When the slopes caught fire, which happened more and more often, Santa Barbara residents would hear on the news that firefighters had to wait until evening for the winds to die down. Of course, by then homes would have burned. The other type, the famed Santa Ana winds, are also hot, dry, and descend slopes, but they come from the Great Basin and affect a much larger area. Sometimes the sundowners would hit and then a few days later the Santa Anas would show up to finish the job.

Between 1955 and the 2020s, more than 1 million acres burned in Santa Barbara County in major fires, 41 percent of its total acreage.

And fifteen of those twenty fires occurred since 1990. The Thomas Fire in December 2017 consumed 282,000 acres, making it the largest in the state's history. Then the next summer came the Mendocino Complex Fire to the north, which burned 460,000 acres, breaking the six-month-old state record. And remember this was when global warming was just getting started, when deniers were still claiming that the wildfires were happening because the U.S. Forest Service refused to clear the debris and dead trees that provided the fuel.

Every thinking person knew that this was going to be the Century of Fire in California. Wildfires have become a constant fact of life, filling the air with smoke, which never seems to completely go away. Much of our national forest acreage has burned, as have many of the small towns on the outskirts of the forest.

One of the most dangerous aspects of California fires is what happens after them, especially in chaparral country. Fires burn the vegetation whose roots hold the soil together, so that the next downpour can dislodge soil, rocks, and the fire debris, entraining them and sending them downslope onto whatever lies below. These debris flows can pick up speed as they travel, much like an avalanche. If they hit a populated area, removal of the debris can take years and cost more than the fire damage itself. This exact scenario happened to our beautiful community of Montecito, when in 2018 debris flows up to 15 feet [4.5 meters] high and traveling at 20 miles per hour [32 kph] destroyed one hundred homes and killed twenty-one people. It buried the critical 101 highway under mud and rock that took months to clear.

So far, I have been talking about the largest fires, ones that burned hundreds of thousands of acres—the ones that attract our attention. Of course, the vast majority of fires are smaller, but they too destroy homes and lives before firefighters can put them out. My grandparents nearly lost their home to one of those back in 2018—the Holiday Fire, named after one of the streets. At 113 acres, it paled by comparison to the gigantic Thomas Fire. Nevertheless, the Holiday Fire destroyed ten homes, nearly including my grandparents', and cost $1.5 million to fight. These small fires became much more common, to the point that two or more would happen at the same time, while the firefighters had the resources to fight only one. This used to be less of a problem because when a fire broke out in one area, fire departments from across the state and even beyond would rush to give assistance. But increasingly, fire departments grew reluctant to leave their area of responsibility for fear that a fire would break out there and get out of control before they could get back to fight it.

In my files I have a fire map from 2020 that showed where each part of the state had burned since 1950. It displayed the fire areas in different colors by year and the unburned areas in white. There had been so many that the map looked like a patchwork quilt. Still, some areas had been largely spared—the Central Valley, for example, where there was little timber to sustain a large fire. One fire zone ran southeast down the east side of the state where the national parks and forests are found, another came down the coastal range to the west of the Central Valley. Below Bakersfield, the two zones met and continued south as one all the way to the Mexican border. When I studied this map early in my career, it was obvious that it showed where conditions were favorable to fire and thus where future fires were most likely to hit.

If we were to update the map now, some counties would have no unburned areas left. Those that the map showed had burned often would by now have burned again, requiring different patterns to be used in addition to the colors to make the map legible. Our neighbor Ventura County already showed these patterns in the old map, as well as a sliver of white. Now it would show solid color from county line to county line, with colors and patterns laid on top of each other. Really, today the Ventura County map would need 3-D layers so you could tell the fires apart.

Before we wind up, tell me how the California fires affected its two big power companies.

In a nutshell, fire put them out of business. Most California fires were caused by humans, rather than lightning. And most of the human-caused ones were down to defective power company equipment of one sort or another. Power lines short out and spark, wires can touch a poorly trimmed and dried-out tree branch and start a fire. It is really stunning to think that such huge fires can start from a handful of sparks in the wrong place.

California law required power companies to reimburse home-owners for damage due to their equipment. The companies also got sued by consumer groups for amounts totaling in the tens of billions. Both the two big California power companies, Pacific Gas and Electric and Southern California Edison, had their bonds downgraded to junk and declared bankruptcy. Both went out of business in the 2020s and the state had to try to become the power supplier. Private utility companies became one more victim of global warming.

People used to say that fire was the new normal in California. We scientists did not care for that phrase, because it implied that the world had gone from one stable level to another. Instead, there is a new normal every year. I suppose the concept plays into our inherent desire to believe that if we can only get through a period of change, we will arrive at a new period of stability to which we can then adapt. But what if there is no longer such a thing as normal, if change itself has become normal?

The future of fire in California and the future of sea level rise differ in one macabre way. At some point, much of what can burn will have burned and the number of new fires and acres burned will peak and begin to decline, as already seems to be happening. How much of California will be inhabitable by then is anyone's guess. But sea level will just keep right on rising, squeezing Santa Barbara residents into an ever-shrinking habitable zone between sea and mountain slopes. For Santa Barbarans, this is how paradise ends.

PART 2
FLOODING

Dr. Vivien Rosenzweig was director of Columbia University's Center for Climate Systems Research, now located in Poughkeepsie, New York.

Dr. Rosenzweig, I know that you were aware that New York City was vulnerable to the effects of global warming. But did you ever imagine it would cause your center to have to move 75 miles [121 km] up the Hudson River?

We scientists did know that global warming was going to be bad, very bad. But even we were surprised when the extreme weather events that we forecast for the thirties and forties began to show up in the tens and twenties. We had worried that our climate models had not captured every conceivable feedback and it appears we were right. Speaking personally, I never imagined that things in New York City would get so bad that Columbia and other universities would have to close some of their operations and, as we can see today, in many cases close completely. Columbia's trustees had divested of the university's stock in coal companies, but it continued to hold on to stock in Big Oil until it was too late to make a difference. I wish the trustees of the twenties were alive to look around today to see what their policy has wrought. We were lucky to be able to move here, but in this new era, luck is only temporary. The whole thing makes me terribly sad and we need to get to your questions before I become too despondent to have an intelligent conversation.

Yes, we knew that New York City was vulnerable and for two reasons in particular. First, like many cities, New York's public facilities had wound up on land that no one wanted to buy and that was therefore available at low cost. Much of New York's sewage- and water-treatment facilities, for example, were on land only several feet above sea level. Many of the subway lines were below sea level. The three airports had elevations of only 10 to 20 feet [3 to 6 meters], as anyone who flew into LaGuardia Airport before it shut down could not help but notice. When a big storm rode in on top of seas that global warming had made higher, these low-lying but vital public operations would be the first to fail.

The second vulnerability was that New York lay in the path of storms from two different directions: hurricanes moving up from the south and nor'easters moving down from New England. The nor'easters have lower wind speed, but they often stay around longer, giving their floodwaters time to reach farther into city streets and buildings.

Let me review some history. One of the first large recorded storms struck New York in 1821. The eye made a direct hit on the city and in one hour threw up a storm surge of 13 feet [4 meters], flooding lower Manhattan as far north as Canal Street. In 1893, a storm destroyed Hog Island off the southern coast of Long Island. The great storm of 1938, known as the Long Island Express, lifted a wall of water 33 feet [10 meters] high and killed seven hundred people. Then in September 1960, Hurricane Donna, a Category 3 storm, erected a surge of nearly 11 feet [3 meters]. Donna flooded lower Manhattan almost to waist level at what would become the site of the World Trade Center. Airports cut back service and subways and highways closed. In December 1992, a nor'easter hit with winds of 80 miles an hour [130 kph] and wave heights of 20 to 25 feet [6 to 7.5 meters], causing some of the worst flooding in New York's history. Hurricane Floyd, a Category 2 storm, arrived in September 1999 to dump 16 inches [400 mm] of rain in twenty-four hours. Fortunately,

Floyd arrived at low tide and was already weakening, so it did not produce a big storm surge.

What I am reminding us of is that in the twentieth century, New York had already been shown to be susceptible to extreme weather events. As the twenty-first century proceeded, the oceans warmed and, by 2060, caused hurricane intensity to increase so that what had been a Category 3 storm with maximum winds of 130 miles per hour [210 kph] was now likely to be a Category 4, with maximum winds of 155 miles per hour [250 kph].

As you know, we rank floods and other extreme weather events by their frequency. The hundred-year flood has odds of 1 in 100 of happening in a given year. This does not mean that once that flood has happened, you are off the hook for the next ninety-nine. Early in the century, Houston had three so-called five-hundred-year storms in three years. Scientists estimated storm frequency from past experience, but as we found out, with global warming, the past is no longer a sound guide to the future. I want to underscore that and apply it more broadly: Throughout human history, people have estimated risk based on the past. You did not build your home on a known river floodplain nor your beach house too near the highest tideline. When you built an irrigation system, say in the Imperial Valley of California, you assumed that the flow of the Colorado River would vary, but on the average would stay the same. And so on. But by burning fossil fuels, we did away with the past as a guide to the future, to humanity's peril.

As global warming caused sea level and storm intensity to rise and floodwaters and storm surges to reach farther into the city, the hundred-year flood became the fifty-year flood, then the twenty-five-year flood, and now the ten-year flood. It is hard to live and conduct business knowing that a major flood is ten times as likely as it used to be.

The big nor'easter of 2028, named Alphonse, resembled the 1992 nor'easter in that it moved more quickly into the New York area than had been forecast but, once it got there, stalled and poured rain for days. The timing could not have been worse, as the storm came in on a full moon and remained for four flood tides. It shorted out the entire New York City subway system and left people stranded on trains and in stations. Some of the subway stations in lower Manhattan flooded to the ceiling. It took months to remove the salt water and replace shorted and corroded electrical equipment and get the subways operating. The PATH transportation link between New York City and New Jersey had to be shut down for nearly a month. The runways at LaGuardia were under a foot of salt water that took days to drain. Six and a half feet [2 meters] of water covered the FDR Drive, and many other roads in lower Manhattan were flooded. The storm destroyed Fire Island and other low-lying islands, plus many homes in Westhampton and adjoining parts of Long Island. The floodwaters temporarily split lower Manhattan into two islands roughly divided at Canal Street. For more than a week before the water receded, people could reach Wall Street and the rest of the Financial District only by boat. The storm cost $20 billion and took the lives of an estimated three thousand people, more than Hurricane Katrina. But it was only a warning shot.

The big storm did have the benefit of prompting New York City officials to send teams to study the Dutch dikes and sea gates—this was two decades before the Maeslant gates collapsed and let in the water that destroyed Rotterdam. New York began to erect storm-surge barriers at three critical points: the mouth of the Arthur Kill between Staten Island and New Jersey, in the Narrows at the entrance to New York Harbor, and across the upper East River just above LaGuardia Airport. The three barriers would seal off and protect Manhattan, Staten Island, the New Jersey peninsula, and the inland sections of

Brooklyn and Queens. But the plan left the South Shore of Long Island, the Rockaways, Brighton Beach, and JFK Airport unprotected. With twenty-twenty hindsight, we can see that this was a major lesson of the twenty-first century: We can save some people and some areas, but we cannot save everyone, everywhere, every time.

In the Northern Hemisphere, hurricanes have a counterclockwise motion, causing their most destructive winds to lie to the right of the eye. The particular arrangement of sea and land near New York City worsens the potential damage from a large hurricane as these counterclockwise westerlies funnel water through the sharp bend between New Jersey and Long Island and directly into New York Harbor.

By the time the big storm struck in August 2042, the combined effect of the global rise in sea level and the subsiding land in the New York area had made sea level effectively 2 feet [0.6 meters] higher than it had been in 2000. 2042-8 was a Category 3 storm that traveled north over the Atlantic just off the Jersey Shore, and then, as it neared the city, unexpectedly veered a few degrees west, right onto the worst-case track.[2] To this point, the storm had moved over water and avoided the slowing effect of travel over land. It made landfall at Asbury Park and continued north and slightly west over Perth Amboy, Elizabeth, Newark, and Paterson.

The sea barrier between Staten Island and New Jersey as well as the one across the upper East River above LaGuardia were still under construction; within hours they collapsed. The barrier at the mouth of New York Harbor by then had been operating successfully for two years. But after twenty-four hours of continual pummeling by 125-mile-per-hour [201 kph] winds and 45-foot [14-meter] storm

[2]   The National Oceanic and Atmospheric Administration (NOAA) used to give hurricanes the first names of people. When they ran out of names, they labeled hurricanes numerically by year hyphen month and the rest of the world adopted the nomenclature.

surges, it too collapsed. The barrier had been built by the Army Corps of Engineers under the assumption that sea level rise by 2100 would be only 1.8 feet [0.55 meters], a level passed in 2050.

A huge surge of water rushed into Upper New York Bay, attacked the base of the Statue of Liberty, and washed over Ellis and Governors Islands, wiping them out. The big waves continued to erode the footing of the statue, until finally one giant wave toppled her. There she lies still, on her side, torch extinguished beneath a sea higher than her builders could have imagined.

The storm surge from 2042-8 destroyed not only the islands in the bay but major parts of the city. A 25-foot [7-meter] surge drowned LaGuardia Airport. At JFK, the water rose 33 feet [10 meters], leaving the airport in ruins. Water flooded the Lincoln Tunnel to its ceiling, drowning hundreds of people in their cars. Huge waves crashed over the Brooklyn Battery Tunnel and surged into the Financial District, flooding the lower meter or two of every building there.

The storm not only left large swaths of Manhattan underwater, it swamped the Rockaways, Coney Island, and other sections of Brooklyn. Parts of Long Island City, Astoria, and Flushing Meadows Park were underwater in Queens, as well as a section of Staten Island from Great Kills Harbor north to the Verrazano Bridge. The entire transportation system failed. Power went out almost immediately throughout the city and took months to restore. People tried to get out of the city by car and on foot, and many died. The scene on the George Washington Bridge resembled that at the World Trade Center disaster in 2001, with bodies falling through the air. Looting was rampant. Police and medical facilities were overwhelmed. New York became something close to an open city and to bring it back under the rule of law took nearly a year.

Remember that the attack on the World Trade Center, even considering the effects of smoke and dust, directly affected only a small part of the city. The storm of 2042 wreaked havoc in a vastly larger area and brought the entire city of New York and its surrounding areas to a halt. Many companies and organizations saw no future on the island and, if they were able, relocated to higher elevations inland, as my center had to do. This, of course, was just the beginning of the worldwide flight from the coasts, where already by midcentury life was becoming untenable.

My center and I are safe here, but what are we supposed to do with our safety? We went into science to make the world a better place, and that is no longer a possibility. What now is our purpose in life?

Harold R. Wanless IV is the great-grandson of a distinguished turn-of-the-century geologist at the University of Miami. The younger Wanless is a specialist on Florida history and also the family genealogist. I reached him at his home 5 miles [8 km] west of Biscayne Bay.

My great-granddad's specialty was coastal geology, giving him insight into how a rise in sea level would affect South Florida. Early in the century, he was asked to chair the science committee of the Miami-Dade County Climate Change Task Force. He knew that the job would take him away from his own research and likely make him the bearer of bad tidings. But he saw the assignment as his civic duty. From reading his letters and articles I can see he believed that if scientists did not speak the truth about what global warming might do to Florida, who would?

The committee's report, which I have in our family files, came out in September 2007. It said that according to the geological evidence, for almost all of the past 2,500 years, sea level in South Florida had been rising at an average of 1.5 inches [38 mm] per century. It was this gradual, slow rise that allowed a stable coastline of mangrove swamps and beaches to develop, which in turn made the Florida coast a relatively secure and safe place to build. Then his panel dropped its bombshell: Since 1932, the rate of sea level rise had accelerated to about one foot [300 mm] per century, roughly eight times the previous, 2,500-year average. The cause of the acceleration, said my great-grandfather and his colleagues, was global warming. Those were bad words in those days. State reports avoided any mention of global warming, as if that would make it go away.

My grandad's committee forecast that sea level would rise at least 1.5 feet [0.5 meters] in the next fifty years and between 3 and 4.5 feet [0.9 and 1.4 meters] by the end of the century. In some yellowed clippings I found him telling our state legislature that a sea-level rise of 4 feet [1.2 meters] would be extremely difficult to live with in South Florida, and 5 feet [1.5 meters] would make life virtually impossible. He said that if sea level rose by 3.3 feet [1 meter], "freshwater resources would be gone; seawater would inundate the Everglades on the west side of Miami-Dade County; the barrier islands would be largely swamped; storm surges would be devastating; landfill sites would be exposed to erosion, contaminating marine and coastal environments." Each of these predictions has come true, but did anyone listen?

If you will pardon this aside, in my view, at that time Florida had a government and a congressional delegation that included several science deniers. Yet all had sworn the same oath—I will read it:

> I do solemnly swear (or affirm) that I will support, protect, and defend the Constitution and Government of the United States and of the State of Florida; that I am duly qualified to hold office under the Constitution of the State, and that I will well and faithfully perform the duties on which I am now about to enter, so help me God.

The oath does not specifically mention the welfare of the people, but only because that was understood, it didn't have to be stated. We have militaries not because we know war is coming, but in case it does, which history shows often happens. We look ahead, we prepare for possible futures. But Florida officials did not do that—they said they were right about the future and the global community of scientists was wrong.

The forecast from my great-grandfather's group was especially alarming when you remember the things that made Florida attractive in the first place back then: the weather, the beaches, and the scenery. His committee had become convinced that global warming would jeopardize all three. If Florida became too hot for people to enjoy the outdoors, if its beaches shrank beneath higher seas, if the Everglades were drowned, and if the northern climate became warmer, making it less necessary for people to fly south with the snowbirds—would they still want to come to Florida? We have since found out that they didn't, and they don't.

As this century wore on, we Floridians noticed that high tides gradually pushed water farther and farther inland. Each time we visited our favorite beach, it was narrower. In the Everglades, water rose until most of the area west of Miami was underwater. Hurricanes grew noticeably stronger. Then there was the heat. Floridians were used to it, but the extreme days became almost unbearable. An article in the *Miami Herald* reported that Miami's temperature in 2035 would have made it one of the hottest cities in the world in 2000—not to mention its humidity. To be outside nowadays is to risk your health or worse. Personally, what I find hardest to take is that it never cools off at night anymore. I used to like sitting on my patio and enjoying a cool evening sea breeze after the sun went down, sipping my rum and tonic when you could still get rum. No more. We still go out to our patios, because, with electricity rationed, most of us can't afford to run air conditioners, but sitting outside is not much better than staying in.

In 2056, South Florida had its Big One.

It was the final blow, no pun intended. It was a Category 4 storm known as 2056-8 that made a direct hit on Miami Beach and sent a 33-foot [10-meter] storm surge sweeping inland. The waves cut a half-mile [0.8 km] swath that destroyed the Miami Beach Golf Club, the marina, and overtopped many buildings. Afterward, Miami Beach had two barrier islands where one had been before and the Atlantic had a direct path into Biscayne Bay. Fisher and Dodge Islands were underwater; beaches from Fort Lauderdale south through Hollywood, Miami Beach, and Key Biscayne were gone.

The Port of Miami had been one of the world's largest, but 2056-8 destroyed the Lummus Island cargo-container facility and flooded the rest of the port beyond repair. That left Miami with no way to handle cargo ships; remember that by that time the cruise industry had long been shut down.

As sea level continued to rise, Key West International Airport flooded. The water threatened to inundate Highway 1, making it likely that before long Key West would be cut off from the mainland and reachable only by boat. That started an exodus that left Key West a ghost town.

The spring high tides pushed farther inland, often flooding the backside of the barrier islands. On the mainland, drainage became more sluggish and salt stunted many South Florida crops. We had to abandon the Turkey Point Nuclear Generating Station and Homestead Air Reserve Base, both on low-lying land near Homestead. Turkey Point was the sixth-largest power plant in the United States and its loss caused electricity rationing.

The South Florida business and real estate climate went from boom to bust. People just walked away from their mortgaged homes, leaving the keys in the mailbox. You can walk around abandoned neighborhoods now and sometimes open a mailbox and find those old, rusty keys still in there.

By last year, sea level had risen by 3.9 feet [1.2 meters], within the range of my great-grandfather's prediction. All along the Atlantic

coast of Florida, much of the land behind the beachfront and border-
ing the inner lagoons is underwater. Miami Beach is gone. Cities like
Fort Lauderdale and Vero Beach have lost more than half their land,
and people are abandoning the rest as fast as they can.

You don't have time for me to discuss more than a small part of
what happened to South Florida and Miami—let me focus on one
section, Miami's crown jewel, the Brickell District. Early in the century, construction in Brickell had given Miami a new skyline. The area
housed the financial district, luxury high-rise condos, tall office towers, mansions, and the like. Brickell was "the Manhattan of the South,"
or "Millionaires' Row." But today, from the Miami River south to the
Rickenbacker Causeway and inland for 2 miles [3 km], the ground
floor of every building in Brickell is underwater. All the corporate
headquarters, the four-star hotels, the luxury condominiums have
closed, leaving their derelict buildings to decay from the ground up.

Of course, Brickell sat right on the shores of Biscayne Bay, barely
above sea level. Inland a few miles, the land is still several feet above
it. But imagine yourself living where I do, a few miles west of Homestead. To the immediate west lie the Everglades, so we can't escape
in that direction. If I ride my bike east toward the coast, I see more
abandoned homes and businesses the farther I ride, and more standing water stranded by the highest tides. I know that only a few miles
farther and I will come to Miami Beach and Brickell, flooded by permanent seawater several feet deep. The scientists tell us that the sea is
going to continue to rise for the rest of this century and well into the
next—no one can say how much or how long. At some point, a storm
surge riding on those higher seas is going to reach my property, or
maybe it will be my children's if for some foolish reason they decided
to stick around. It's inevitable, isn't it? What would any sane person
do? If there was any way, get out. And most have. We Wanlesses, a

long line of proud Floridians, have stuck it out as long as we can, but we will soon be on the road with what possessions we can haul, going where, I am not sure. In twenty or thirty years, South Florida will be almost completely depopulated and sometime a century or so from now, underwater, returned to the sea from which it emerged. They should have listened to my great-grandad.

BANGLADESH: GEOGRAPHY AS DESTINY

In the early years of the century, scientists predicted that three countries would be especially vulnerable to the coming rise in sea level: Egypt, Vietnam, and Bangladesh. To learn about the twenty-first-century history of Bangladesh, I speak with Dr. Mohammad Rahman, a meteorologist now in his eighties. Dr. Rahman spoke with me from his office in Dhaka. Like most Bangladeshis of his generation, he spoke excellent English.

You must pardon me if a note of anger creeps into my responses. It is hard to be a Bangladeshi in the 2080s and not feel anger, especially toward you first-world countries, as you used to call yourselves. First at what: ruining the world for everyone else? How many Westerners know the slightest thing about our history, or care? How many knew that by the 2020s the economy of Bangladesh was rising sharply, and our standard of living was improving? Then came the global warming that you caused.

No country better proves your English expression, "Geography is destiny." Bangladesh is squeezed between two unforgiving forces of nature: to the north loom the high Himalayas, home to the tallest mountains on Earth and the glaciers and snowfields that feed the great rivers that flow down to the sea. To the south lies the Bay of Bengal of the northern Indian Ocean, home to the deadliest cyclones on Earth.

Bangladesh's rivers carry massive amounts of sediment eroded from the Himalayan slopes. When they reach the lowlands, the rivers dump the silt to create the world's largest delta, a vast coastal plain of low slope and elevation. At the turn of the century, 80 percent of Bangladesh was less than 33 feet [10 meters] above sea level and 20 percent was less than 3.3 feet [1 meter] above. Imagine if, when this century began, one-fifth of the United States had been less than one meter above sea level! Your politicians would have sung a different tune. We Bangladeshis had so many rivers and creeks that we used to have a saying, which I will translate: "There is not a single village without a river or a rivulet and a folk poet or a minstrel." Now our rivers have dried up and our poets and troubadours have fallen silent.

You may be surprised to learn that in 2000, including us Bangladeshis, 1.3 billion people lived in the drainage basins of ten great rivers originating in the Himalayas. The melting Himalayan glaciers fed the Ganges and Brahmaputra, which supplied much of Bangladesh's water. Climate scientists told us that mountains would warm faster than the plains, and they were right. Early in the century, glaciers in the high Himalayas were retreating by 59 to 66 feet [18 to 20 meters] each year. The Mingyong Glacier on Mount Kawagebo, one of Tibetan Buddhism's eight sacred peaks, was one of the fastest-shrinking in the world. Until about 2040, due to the faster rate of melting, the glacier-fed rivers that drain the southern flank of the Himalayas ran higher than ever in history, making floods our immediate concern. But as the glaciers continued to melt and shrink, they began to send less and less meltwater down the rivers each year, and we had the opposite problem. Today, both the Ganges and Brahmaputra run dry for months each year, sharply cutting freshwater supplies and adding to the tens of millions of Bangladeshi climate refugees. This cycle of first flood and then drought has been repeated wherever nations depended on rivers fed by glacial meltwater. No doubt you will interview others with the same sad story.

By 2050, global sea level had risen almost 3.3 feet [1 meter]. Because so much of our land was close to sea level, the rise and the higher storm surges had cost Bangladesh one-fourth of its territory.

The tropical cyclones (you call them hurricanes) had grown more intense and reached much farther inland. The higher sea level and storm surges not only caused more damage and death, they allowed salt water to contaminate our groundwater. We often had to abandon fields as far as 25 miles [40 km] from the coast. The loss of land to erosion and the poisoning by salt water cut our rice production by two-thirds. Crops had also failed in Australia and other countries in Southeast Asia, leaving rice unavailable for import even had we the money to buy it—and rice is the staple of the Bangladeshi diet. Widespread famine followed, and many tried to leave Bangladesh, believing, or hoping against hope, that India and other neighbors would take them in.

Even before the Great Warming, floods and storms had displaced up to 6 million Bangladeshis each year. Many emigrated illegally to overcrowded shantytowns in India. At first the Indian government turned a blind eye. But as the numbers rose, in the 1980s India built its own "Great Wall," a 2,540-mile [4,100-km] steel fence along its entire border with Bangladesh. Perhaps this is where the U.S. government long ago got the ignorant and unworkable idea to build a barricade along your border with Mexico. The India-Bangladeshi wall cost a great deal of money and had little effect. I doubt such barriers can ever keep desperate people out. But certainly no wall of any kind could withstand the onslaught—the literal pressure—of hundreds of thousands, even millions, of climate refugees for whom in this century crossing a border became not just a route to a better life but to having a life at all.

By midcentury there were 25 million Bangladeshi climate refugees; today there are estimated to be 50 million, and the number continues to rise. Most have no way to earn an income, no place to live except in the lethal refugee camps. The poor water quality, rising temperatures, increased numbers of disease-carrying mosquitoes, and insufferable sanitary conditions caused outbreaks of cholera, dysentery, typhus, and yellow fever. For a while, your country and others sent aid, but, as the years went by, you no longer had the money or interest to send aid halfway around the world. International aid agencies like the Red Cross, Red Crescent, and Médecins Sans Frontières have long since closed their doors. In this century, it is every nation for itself and, as you say, the devil take the hindmost—and the hindmost seems to be the Bangladeshi people.

Our population peaked at 170 million people in 2025, and, though no one knows how many remain, experts believe that today we have fewer than 75 million. What should we call what has happened to Bangladesh and the world? We cannot use the word "genocide," for all nations and races have suffered and global warming was not intentional. But neither can we say it was accidental. The nations of the world had fair warning, yet their leaders stood by and let it happen. Not just the first-world nations but countries like our neighbors China and India—all failed.

You Americans cannot deny you knew what would happen to Bangladesh when the big cyclones arrived on the higher seas of the warmer Earth. In December 2008, over seventy-five years ago, your National Defense University held an exercise examining the potential effects of large floods that would send hundreds of thousands of Bangladeshi refugees into India. The study forecast that the result would be religious conflict, the spread of contagious diseases, and widespread damage to infrastructure, the very things that have happened. But you did not intend your exercise to show how to protect Bangladesh; rather it was to determine the strategic implications of such floods on the U.S., as though we were mice in your laboratory cages. Those who were largely responsible for global warming simply washed their hands of those of us in what you derided as "the third world." Our blood stains your hands, and time will never wash away that stain. But now you are getting a taste of the medicine you forced us to swallow.

Dr. Maurice Richard was professor of geology at the University of Louisiana at Lafayette and a leading expert on the history of New Orleans and its floods. His Cajun family came to the area west of New Orleans in 1765, after Le Grand Dérangement that followed the French and Indian War. We met on a boat tour of the ruins of New Orleans.

Dr. Richard, much of New Orleans is permanently underwater. Even though the city's founders could not have foreseen global warming, it is hard today to understand why they ever regarded the mouth of the Mississippi River as a safe place to build a great city.

Remember that the people who settled America had no history on the continent themselves nor any written history to draw on. They had little idea how often the Mississippi flooded and how often hurricanes struck. Even if they had known, they still would have assumed that the river and the Gulf would behave in the future as they had in the past. The Mississippi River would run high in some years and low in others but would stay within its historical boundaries. Wetlands would continue to protect southern Louisiana against storm surges. There would be extreme high tides and low ones, but the sea would settle back and over the long run, mean sea level would stay the same. *Plus ça change, plus c'est la même chose.* Today we wish that saying were still true.

To the Native Americans and early settlers on this continent, a delta had many advantages: a continual supply of water; exceptionally fertile soil; access to the ocean downstream and to river settlements upstream; abundant fish and shellfish; and so on. That is how we got not only New Orleans but Alexandria, Belém, Rangoon, Rotterdam, Saigon, Shanghai, Tianjin, and the like. Yet deltas were always risky places to build, threatened by floodwaters moving downstream, tidal surges moving upstream, and land that continually subsided, kept above water only by new silt arriving from upstream.

But new silt does not wind up in the same place as the old. In a delta, new channels constantly form and old ones close, so that a delta's landscape is always changing. But a city cannot live with shifting channels and wandering silt. A city needs its river and silt to stay in one place, so it builds levees to imprison the river in its channel. The river becomes a prisoner, but one with unlimited time and energy. It never stops trying to escape; not this year, not next year, and not in the next ten thousand years. However long it takes, the river will break out. To keep such an escape artist locked up even temporarily, the wardens cannot let down their guard for a second. To change metaphors midstream, to build a city on a delta is to bet that you can beat nature at her game and do so indefinitely. That is a bet you are bound to lose.

People who had not thought much about the consequences of a rising sea seemed to imagine that the main effect would be that instead of the water on your favorite beach coming up to your ankles, say, under global warming it would come up to your knees. How bad was that? But delta land often slopes by no more than 1 percent: 1 foot vertically for each 100 feet [30 meters] of lateral distance. On that kind of grade, by the time water has risen to your knees it will have extended inland by another 150 feet [45 meters]. The beach shrinks and in time disappears. Then higher storm surges push the sea even farther inland. People should have focused not only on the vertical rise of sea level, but also on how much farther the higher seas would push water inland and what the effect would be on coastal cities.

What was it about New Orleans that made it particularly vulnerable?

Its location on a delta was one strike against New Orleans. But it had two others. Consider the family of big storms that struck the Gulf Coast just in the second half of the twentieth century—Flossy, Betsy, Camille, Juan, Andrew, and Georges. New Orleans lay in a major hurricane zone and scientists had predicted that this century storms would grow stronger, and they did.

Lake Pontchartrain, which formed the northern boundary of New Orleans, was the third strike. The lake was only about 13 feet [4 meters] deep and its surface was just above sea level, so it was vulnerable to storm waters surging in from the nearby Gulf of Mexico. In the old days, levees kept the lake water from sloshing down into the city. But Lake Pontchartrain was a disaster waiting to happen.

Back in 2005 a hurricane struck that people feared was the Big One, though it made landfall only as a Category 3. Hurricane Katrina damaged New Orleans so badly that some, including the Speaker of the House of Representatives, said America should just abandon the city. But that was never in the cards. To give up on one of its most historic cities was simply not in the American spirit. Presidents and senators had no choice but to promise to rebuild New Orleans better than ever.

By 2015, the Army Corps of Engineers had spent nearly $15 billion to repair levees and build new structures to protect New Orleans. All in the name of "flood protection," which some had begun to call the new oxymoron, like airline cuisine or jumbo shrimp.

The population of the New Orleans metro area declined in the immediate aftermath of Katrina, but then, partly because of the promised protections, recovered close to what it had been. I have an old newspaper article from back then that quotes one of New Orleans's famous singers, Irma Thomas, summing up the attitude of its stubborn residents: "When you move to New Orleans, you know it's below sea level. You know it's like a fishbowl, and you know the possibilities. So you make up your mind that this is where you want to live."

None of the geologic and hydrologic facts of life on a delta had changed—they change only on a geologic time scale, not a human one. The Mississippi River delta continued to shrink and subside, largely because upstream dams trapped more than half the silt that had once come down the Big Muddy. The high-banked levees prevented the silt from spreading out and replenishing the delta, instead carrying the sediment right out to the edge of the continental shelf and dumping it in the Gulf, where it did New Orleans no good. An acre of southern Louisiana wetlands continued to disappear every twenty-four minutes.

During the twentieth century, New Orleans had sunk by 3 feet [1 meter] and in this century, it continued to sink. Land sinking, sea level rising—a fatal combination. Back at the turn of the century, scientists at LSU had projected that by 2090, the Gulf Coast would have advanced northward until it passed the center of New Orleans. In other words, after that date, New Orleans would be part of the Gulf of Mexico, not part of Louisiana. The constant threat, or, as some realists saw it, the inevitability, was that on top of the rise of the sea and the sinking of the delta, another hurricane was bound to arrive and deliver New Orleans its coup de grâce. You can see by looking around you that these predictions were mostly right.

The dreaded storm struck in mid-September 2048. Had it hit even a few decades earlier, when the waters of the Gulf were cooler, it would have likely ranked as a Category 2 instead of the Category 4 to which the warmer seas had promoted it. Sea level would have been lower and more of the wetlands and barrier islands would have been present to protect the city.

Beginning life as a Category 2, Hurricane 2048-9 followed a path familiar to hurricane buffs since it followed the track of a Category 4 storm that had hit New Orleans way back in 1915. Like that storm, 2048-9 first drew attention near Puerto Rico. As it moved west, like most Gulf hurricanes the storm began to swing north. It passed midway between western Cuba and the Yucatán and before long the warmer Gulf waters had strengthened it to a Category 4. Forecasters predicted that there was a fifty-fifty chance it would make a direct hit on New Orleans. The storm made landfall just east of Atchafalaya Bay and continued on a northeasterly course, the eye passing some 15 miles [24 km] west of the center of the city. Driven by 155 mile-per-hour [250 kph] winds, storm waters surged inland to the edge of New Orleans, and, in some cases, into it. Many of the supposedly strengthened levees failed and many districts flooded. Lake Pontchartrain overflowed its western edge and spilled south into the downtown area, drowning New Orleans under several feet of water.

The drowning of New Orleans had a major psychological effect around the world. Its fate showed that any port city severely damaged by flooding would have to be abandoned, since another storm, as great or greater, was bound to strike. As the seas rose, the money *and the confidence*—please emphasize those words—to rebuild coastal cities dried up. To many, if New Orleans could not survive, then neither could life on the seacoast anywhere. As always, the significance of the Big Easy outranked its size. There will never be another like it.

Wang Wei is a retired engineer who in 2032 was working at China's im-mense Three Gorges Dam in Hubei Province when insurgents took out the dam and caused the greatest flood in human history. I interviewed Wang at his daughter's home in Chongqing.

Engineer Wang, tell us about the history of the Three Gorges Dam and the Uighur attack.

I started my career at the dam right after I earned my master's degree from your University of Southern California in 2025. Three Gorges Dam had been finished in 2006 and at the time was the biggest project ever built in China. The dam was 7,660 feet [2,335 meters] long—about a mile and a half—and when it was full the reservoir held 10,000 trillion gallons [32 million acre-feet]. Three Gorges was a candidate for the largest project ever built by man and the source of immense national pride in China. To work there was the dream of any Chinese engineer.

At the time of construction, Chinese officials said the dam had cost $25 billion in U.S. dollars and required the government to relocate 2 million people, but we insiders suspected the real cost to have been close to $100 billion and the number relocated around 20 million.

Something so large was bound to affect the environment. So, it was no surprise to us engineers that thousands of landslides began to occur on the steep hillsides above the dam. We thought that the pressure of the vast amount of water had destabilized the ground and caused the slumping. We feared that an earthquake would cause larger landslides to fall into the reservoir and displace water that would overtop the dam, possibly destroying it directly. In our classes we had studied something like this with your Glen Canyon Dam, when its spillways failed and the dam could have collapsed, wiping out everything downstream it if had. Some of us Chinese students even visited the Grand Canyon and saw the dam, one of the highlights of my time in the States.

Xinjiang, home to the Uighurs, is one of the most isolated places on Earth. The capital city of Urumqi lies farther from the ocean than any large city in the world. The province is also one of the driest places. Without the Tarim River, most of Xinjiang would be too dry to inhabit. And without mountain snow and glaciers, the Tarim would not exist, for a river in a desert cannot get enough water from rain to sustain itself. Melting glaciers in the Kunlun and Tian Shan Mountains circle the Tarim Basin, providing most of the water the river carries. Even in the first decade of this century, the Tarim was already shrinking and of its nine tributaries, by 2010 only three were still flowing and two of them dried up completely for part of the year. Some of the desert-dwelling Uighurs began to tap groundwater aquifers, a strategy that can work only temporarily. People always take out much more water than there is rainfall to replace it, causing the water table to fall, requiring ever larger and more expensive pumps to get the water up to the surface. Thus, from the Uighur point of view, global warming was causing the rivers to dry up, while the groundwater they needed to replace it was sinking out of reach.

Then to make matters worse for them, I am ashamed to say that our authorities began to cut the amount of groundwater that we allowed the Uighurs. If you were a Uighur farmer or business owner, you got less water than your Chinese neighbor. This unfairness caused unrest in the Uighur communities.

By the 2030s, Chinese authorities had more to worry about than the Uighurs. We had ignored international pressure to lower greenhouse gas emissions and while we were talking the talk as you say, we had opened a new coal-burning plant each week. That made our already terrible air pollution worse. In Beijing in the early years of the century, sometimes you could not see the tops of tall buildings, then not even to the end of the block ahead, and eventually not even your shoes. The death rate from respiratory illnesses shot up and people were afraid to leave their homes. In addition to the coal smoke, fine dust particles blew in from the desert to the west of Beijing, making the air quality worse. Some of those particles blew all the way across the Pacific and landed in your Rocky Mountains, where they absorbed heat and made the snow melt faster. And still Chinese people had the highest rate of smoking of any country. Our overall mortality rate began to shoot up, as though we had a five-year plan to poison ourselves.

But I am getting away from my story. In old age, the mind wanders. What I am trying to say is that as time went on, the Chinese government could not afford to spend too much time and resources on the Uighurs. Xinjiang was a long way from Beijing, was running out of water, and was an inhospitable land in the first place. Global warming had turned out to be the greatest threat, or so we thought.

Remember that global warming caused the Himalayan glaciers to melt rapidly in the early years of the century, so that the Yangtze and other Chinese rivers actually ran higher. By the end of the rainy season in 2032, the Three Gorges Reservoir was full to the brim from the icy meltwater. Our security forces increased their vigilance, fearing that someone might try to blow up the dam. But a small group of Uighur rebels were too smart for such a direct attack.

We saw no reason to guard the steep hills that bordered the reservoir above the dam. No one was interested in them except the engineers and geologists trying to predict when and where the next landslide would occur—or so we thought. No one noticed the new-comers who had shown up in the hills above Three Gorges.

What were the rebels up to? One night in September 2032, we found out. They had placed scores of hidden dynamite charges at stra-tegic points on the most unstable slopes above the dam. They shot off all the dynamite at once, the blast waking us engineers in our sleep-ing quarters in Sandouping, a few miles away from the dam. Our first thought was that someone had indeed tried to blow up the dam itself, but a telephone call ended that fear.

The dynamite explosions caused hundreds of landslides and indirectly dislodged many more where the hillsides were already unstable. Millions of tons of rock and soil fell into the brimful res-ervoir. A wave over 330 feet [100 meters] high went surging up and down the length of the reservoir, like water sloshing in a bathtub of giants.

Remember that Three Gorges Dam was the largest hydropower dam in the world and was located on the third-longest river in the world. Its construction required many experimental technologies, including the world's largest submerged spillways. Our engineers could not test all those technologies in advance—often we had to wait for experience to provide the test. No one knew how well the spillways would hold up if they ever had to pass their maximum volumes. Even before the wave of water from the attack reached the dam, the high water that summer had caused the operators to open the spillway gates to their maximum. But then the spillways began to boom and vibrate so much that the operators feared they might rip apart and collapse. So, they had to partially close the spillways and let less water out. That was the exact moment the rebels had been waiting for: a full reservoir with its spillways partially closed.

As the waves from the explosions arrived at the dam, there was no room in the spillways for the extra water, which piled up and then began to crest the dam. Since the spillways were supposed to prevent the reservoir from overflowing, there were no other engineering works to protect the top of the dam. The water washing over the dam immediately destroyed the power plant and then began to pick away at what evidently had been a weak spot in the concrete dam face. The entire world watched the event on television. It was a terrible moment for the Chinese, no doubt the worst moment in a country with a history of natural disasters.

The weak spot turned into a crack, growing wider and deeper, allowing more water to flow through and more erosion to take place— all this was happening in minutes. Soon the crack reached the bottom of the dam face and a chunk of the Three Gorges Dam as tall as a twenty-five-story building broke away and fell into the Yangtze below. Now there was nothing to hold back the ten trillion gallons of water in the reservoir and it began to pour through the cleft and rush downstream.

A giant wall of water washed down the Yangtze, sweeping away everything before it. As the wave took out each successive downstream dam, it rose higher. It spread out as it flowed through the plains but rose higher again as it passed through narrow downstream gorges. The wave destroyed Wuhan, Nanjing, and much of the inland regions of Shanghai. The estimated death toll was 100 million but the damage to China's infrastructure and morale was incalculable.

In addition to the terrible loss of life and property, the destruction of the Three Gorges Dam had another unfortunate consequence: Without the hydropower it had produced, China had to rely even more on coal, causing even more pollution and health problems. The actions of a small group of rebels were used as an excuse for a pogrom against the Uighurs. The government rounded them up by the tens of thousands—men, women, and children—and sent them to death camps where they starved or were executed. By 2040, there was barely an Uighur left alive in China.

PART 3
SEA LEVEL RISE

Dr. Anwar Shindy is an Alexandrian and the former Egyptian minister of antiquities. I spoke with him at his home in Aswan.

Dr. Shindy, how long had your family been in Alexandria?

Our family had lived there continuously since the twelfth century AD. We were merchants, though in the last century some of us got college educations and went into the professions. Alexander the Great founded the city in 331 BC and named it after himself. In ancient times, Alexandria was the link between the civilizations of Greece and Egypt. Cleopatra was born there. At its height, the city was second only to Rome in power and architectural wonders. Perhaps the greatest and most widely known was one of the ancient world's seven wonders: the Lighthouse of Alexandria, on the island of Pharos, with a statue of Helios on top. For centuries it was the tallest structure in the world after our world-famous pyramids. But a tall building invites natural enemies, and in the fourteenth century two great earthquakes brought the lighthouse down. Alexandria also boasted the greatest library of the ancient world, but fire destroyed it.

Greeks, Romans, Persians, French, Britons, and Arabs have assaulted Alexandria, but always we outlasted them. We knew natural disasters and human conquerors; now the sea threatens to become the one conqueror that we cannot outlast.

By the year 2000, Alexandria was the second-largest city in Egypt and housed almost half the country's industrial production. Nearly four million people lived there and another million arrived in the summer to enjoy its beaches and warm Mediterranean waters. But as so many coastal cities have learned, Alex was safe only so long as the sea stayed put, where it had always been even back to antiquity.

Like other delta cities such as your New Orleans, Alexandria lay partly below sea level, protected by levees and breakwaters. The Aswan Dam trapped 90 percent of the silt moving down the upper Nile, starving the delta and causing it to subside, again like New Orleans. As the land sank and the sea rose, saltwater and storm surges reached farther inland, a now familiar story around the world.

At the beginning of this century, experts judged Egypt to be one of the countries most vulnerable to global warming. To understand Alexandria's exposure you needed only a topographic map that showed the 3-foot [1-meter] contour. Our scientists told us that the Mediterranean Sea would rise by that much sometime near the end of the century, and it passed that point two years ago. Salt water now covers the seaward third of Alexandria. Nearly 2 million people have evacuated, mostly to Cairo, which was already so overpopulated as to be nearly unlivable. I preferred Aswan, closer to the source of our antiquities.

From your reading of history, how did the people of Alexandria react when told that sea level would rise by 3 feet [1 meter] by 2100?

First, they denied global warming. As in your country, many laypeople and some demagogues said it was a hoax. In any case, what could we Egyptians have done to prevent it? We produced barely more than half of 1 percent of all CO_2 emissions, so even shutting down our country entirely would have made no difference on a global scale. Someone calculated back then that China emitted as much in ten days as Egypt did in one year.

When carbon dioxide, temperature, and sea level had all risen enough to show that global warming was real and that the Mediterranean was going to rise and invade Alexandria, Egyptians turned angry, especially at the true polluters: the United States, China, India, and the others. Even though it made no sense, some of our most extreme clerics preached that global warming was a holocaust deliberately perpetrated on Muslim and Arabic countries by the Great Satan, the United States. Global warming proved to be an even greater recruitment tool for terrorist organizations than America's wars in Iraq, Afghanistan, Syria, and Iran. Of course, as the century went on, international travel became so difficult that terrorists could no longer move between countries as they once did. Many then turned their anger and fanaticism inward, on their own leaders. I have to say that many of those cruel dictatorships, like the Saudis, deserved what they got, regardless of the source.

As we Egyptians realized that global warming was happening, that it was going to do what the conquerors of old could not, that we were powerless to prevent it, and that it did not matter whose fault it was, a national depression set in—a pandemic of national defeatism that no thinking person could escape. Every marker of the health of a society got worse: suicide, divorce, addiction, murder, and other crimes. Bankruptcy rates rose and life expectancy fell. A terrible, terminal hopelessness settled over Egypt. What really destroyed our spirit was the growing realization that as bad as things were, they were going to get worse. Sea level was not going to stop rising in 2100—no scientist or supercomputer could say when it would. We knew that New Orleans was mostly underwater. What could prevent the same thing from happening to Alexandria?

Of course, everyone everywhere has had to go through this same cycle of emotions. One of your psychologists wrote long ago that there were five stages of grief; I think they were, denial, anger, bargaining, depression, and acceptance. We can now merge the last two, because to accept what is coming is to make depression the normal human condition.

Alexandria and Egypt herself have survived far longer than most cities and nations. But we have finally met a foe whom we know will defeat us. Invisible molecules in the air are conquering what even the Caesars could not.

I meet today with Dr. Ted Black, professor of coastal geography at the University of South Carolina, prior to its closure in 2060 due to failed tax revenue. I have divided this long interview into two chapters.

Dr. Black, I know that your family has deep roots in South Carolina and in Myrtle Beach. Take me back to what drew your family and so many others to the Atlantic seacoast.

Yes, our roots go back a long way. Let me begin by saying that I'm glad to talk to you about our experience even though it is painful. Myrtle Beach is a case study—or as people used to say, the poster child—of the flight from the seacoast that has marked the second half of this century and is literally changing the map of the world.

Since antiquity, people have always wanted to live near the sea. In ancient times it was for practical reasons: the availability of fish, often a moderate climate, and, once the Vikings showed us how to sail out of sight of land and return home, as a place to launch seagoing boats. Early in this century, roughly half the global population lived within about 60 miles [100 km] of the coast, the very places that sea level rise would endanger.

Up through the last century, people who chose to live on the coasts had no way of knowing that the past would never again be a good guide to the future. They reasonably thought that sea level would rise and fall, as it always had, but over the long run, it would return to its long-term average. That said, you have to wonder whether, even if people had known the sea would just keep rising, it would have made any difference. After all, people have always built on floodplains, managing to convince themselves that another flood would not happen in their lifetime, or that if one did, they would survive it.

Five generations ago in 1958, my family bought a beach house in the Garden City section of Myrtle Beach. Family lore has it that the house cost $35,000, a lot of money in those days. The Black House, as we jokingly named it, remained in our family even after my sister and I moved away, me to the university and she to a job with the National Park Service. My father lived in it long after our neighbors had given up and long after he should have sold.

I can sum up the history of Myrtle Beach by saying that by 2025 the value of the house had risen to about $400,000. Then it began to decline, but my father refused to sell. After he died, my sister and I could not find a buyer at any price and just had to walk away from our family home. Looking back at the house as I drove away for the last time is one of those memories as sad as the death of a parent. All those houses in our old neighborhood are gone now, of course.

Perhaps given your family history it was no accident that your academic specialty became coastal geography. Tell me how sea level rose throughout the twentieth and twenty-first centuries and the effect it had on life on the coast.

All right. Let me see if I can approach the subject as a scholar instead of a victim still feeling the pain after all these years.

As the evidence for man-made global warming grew every year, the climate deniers tried to debunk that evidence in any way they could think of. They claimed the rising temperatures were caused by the sun, or that scientists had faked the data, and so on. They said the climate was always changing, that scientists were not in agreement, and a lot of other baloney. But when your favorite beach is half the size it used to be and high tides are creeping farther inland every year, denial is no longer a possibility. Some of our South Carolina politicians also owned beach property and it serves the bastards right.

We know that in the big picture, when the last ice age glaciers began to melt some twenty thousand years ago, sea level eventually rose over 400 feet [120 meters]. That should have given us a hint as to just how dangerous melting polar ice caps and glaciers could be, but of course, our so-called leaders would not only not take a hint, they wouldn't pay attention if you hit them over the head with a two-by-four.

By about six thousand years ago, the melting had mostly ended, and postglacial sea level had stabilized. That lasted until around 1800 and the Industrial Revolution, when carbon dioxide began to spew into the air and raise global temperatures. Sea level began to tick upward again and has not stopped rising since. It will not stop as far out as we can see.

Until the 1990s, scientists measured sea level using tide gauges, but then came satellites, which gave greater coverage and accuracy. The satellite data showed sea level climbing erratically but relentlessly. By 2020 it was rising at about one-tenth of a foot [30 mm] per year, but thanks to the accuracy of the satellite measurements, scientists could tell that the rise was accelerating: growing by more each year than it had the year before. When scientists took the acceleration into account, they projected that by 2100 sea level would have risen by about 2 feet [0.6 meters] above where it stood in 2005.

This reminds me of something related that I need to call out. Back at the turn of the century, projections of the future effects of global warming typically used the year 2100 as their target. That made sense—there had to be a target date and 2100 was the obvious one. But its use created a false impression in the public mind. When scientists said that sea level was going to rise by a certain amount by 2100, most people did not think any further ahead, did not recognize that then it would just keep on rising. Most of us were conditioned to believe that hard times would end and normal times would resume, as happened after the World Wars and Great Depression. The choice of a target date was a dilemma, because if scientists had chosen 2200, say, it would have seemed so far away that we would not have to worry about it. I think of this as one of the many devilish traps of global warming.

Certainly by the 2020s anyone on the South Carolina coast knew they were living with risk. In October 1954, just before my ancestors bought our family home, Hurricane Hazel made a dead hit on Myrtle Beach with wind speeds of more than 100 miles per hour [160 kph]. Hazel struck at the time of the highest astronomical tide, producing a storm surge of 18 feet [5.5 meters], wiping out many parts of the town.

Then for the next thirty-five years, Myrtle Beach had a few Category 1 storms, ones that had started out stronger but had lost wind speed as they traveled over land to get here. Then in September 1989 came Hugo, a Category 4 and the worst storm of the century in South Carolina. Hugo had traveled by sea and picked up speed as it neared the coast, making landfall on the Isle of Palms just northeast of Charleston, only about 95 miles [150 km] from Myrtle Beach.

Hugo destroyed a lot of homes and damaged others, but few people moved as a result. Hurricanes were just a fact of life and, thanks to the National Flood Insurance Program, people had the money to rebuild. I remember my dad telling me that one of our neighbors, an old-timer, had rebuilt four times thanks to that federal money. That program was subsidizing people to live where they wanted to, rather than where they should have. It went broke in the 2020s and Congress canceled it. It should have done so a couple of decades before.

Take us forward from the mid-twenties to the present.

Well, of course, that is the hard part. I'm ashamed that even though I had the scientific knowledge that our neighbors did not, my family still did not act early enough. But my father was never going to move—you would have had to carry him out and sadly that is just what we had to do. I have always been thankful that he did not live to see what happened to our home. It would have killed him if cancer had not.

The first thing to say is that people had plenty of warning about the coming rise in sea level on the Carolina coast. In 2018 the old Union of Concerned Scientists published a study called *Underwater: Rising Seas, Chronic Floods, and the Implications for US Coastal Real Estate*. I dug it out to read before our interview and also found an article on the study from the *Sun News*, which everyone in town read. There is no use in people my age telling their grandchildren that we didn't know. We knew, and they know we knew.

The paper quoted the report as saying that "by 2045, chronic flooding could inundate more than 3,000 homes along the South Carolina coast and low-lying areas." This would cost about $1.4 billion in lost property value and more than $11 million in property taxes. But by 2100, these numbers were projected to rise to more than nineteen thousand homes worth about $6.9 billion. Of course, now we know that those projections, and almost all projections having to do with global warming, were too low.

The question then became what effect such projections and the growing awareness of sea level rise would have on real estate prices and sales. Studies at the time came to different conclusions, some saying that the risk of flooding had already begun to lower home values, others finding no effect. One of the most succinct explanations of what was going on that I have read was that "pessimists began to sell to optimists," an early warning signal of the coming global retreat from the seacoast.

But if I may step out of my area of expertise for a moment, if you look at the big picture of the first three decades, you see that people simply were incapable of receiving bad information and doing anything about it—even when scientists were telling them their grand-children's future was at stake. We claim to be the only species that knows there is a future and can act based on that knowledge, yet we usually don't. The climate deniers kept denying and people kept voting for them, even when their streets had begun to flood.

Dr. Black, let's take a break here and resume tomorrow morning.

Let's pick up again with your family home and the fate of the seacoasts in general.

Buying a house is typically the largest purchase a family ever makes and one that provides their most valuable asset. The purchase of a home requires optimism not only from the buyer but from the lender and insurer as well. It reminds me of what the economist John Maynard Keynes once said about the stock market. He compared it to a newspaper contest that showed photographs of one hundred women and asked readers to pick the six prettiest. (This was in the 1930s, remember.) The winner would be the entrant whose six picks came closest to the average preference of all the readers. Keynes pointed out that the best strategy was not to pick the six faces you thought were the prettiest, but to select the ones you thought other readers would choose. In the same way, trying to gauge what will happen to a given housing market depends not so much on your opinion, but what you think will be the opinion of others. If enough of them believe that sea level is going to rise, or even if they just want to hedge their bets in case it does, they will be less inclined to buy seaside property and if they do so, will make offers below the asking price.

At one time, economists were found of saying, "We are all Keynesians now," meaning that nearly everyone accepted his economic theories. By the 2040s, we were all pessimists about coastal property, which meant there were a lot of sellers but few buyers.

There were a few early signs of change in the Myrtle Beach real

estate market. By the 2020s, GPS-based mapping had become so pre-
cise that buyers, insurance companies, and lenders had a much better
idea of which individual properties were most likely to flood. Anyone
could look on the Internet and see exactly where their house stood
relative to the so-called one-hundred-year-flood elevation. And flood
risk had to be disclosed to prospective buyers. A national study at the
time found that the higher the elevation of beachfront property, the
higher its selling price.

The other early sign of a changing housing market was that sales
of second homes and those owned by investors began to increase—
call the sellers pessimists or call them realists. This was the so-called
smart money, or if not smart, at least not emotionally attached to a
given piece of beachfront property. This began to happen in Myrtle
Beach, and everyone became aware of it from articles in the paper. Attitudes began to change from optimistic to neutral, then to pessimis-
tic. My dad was not the best educated and certainly not the wealthiest.
He had a deep-seated family loyalty to Black House and even though I
pointed these facts out to him, he would never consider selling.

By the twenties, hurricane intensity was already creeping up,
though there did not seem to be more of them. In Myrtle Beach, what
had been a Category 1 storm, the tail end of one that started out stronger but had weakened during its journey over land, was now likely to
arrive as a Cat 1.5 or, increasingly, a Cat 2. As a result, storm surges
reached farther inland, adding a kind of second whammy to the direct
effect of flooded streets and shrinking beaches.

Then in 2030, the local Myrtle Beach paper published a chart
showing (a) the number of homes on the market, (b) the number of
sales, and (c) average sale price, going back to 1990. Category (a) was
rising exponentially, while (b) and (c) were declining in concert. You
could not miss the message: Sell now or risk never being able to sell.

The day after the article came out, people were lined up outside real estate offices, the scene resembling those old grainy black-and-white photos from the Great Depression that showed people queued outside banks hoping to get their money out before the bank failed. Roosevelt wisely declared a Bank Holiday, but the sea takes no holiday.

That article was the beginning of the end for Myrtle Beach. Yet it is surprising that when it appeared, not that many homes had actually been damaged yet. Instead, insurers and lenders had lost confidence, which is just as effective. The federal flood insurance program had been gone for years and private insurers would no longer cover property within the projected twenty-five-year flood line. Without insurance, no lender would finance a mortgage. New construction had stopped several years earlier, and sales of existing homes were falling as the newspaper chart showed. There was hardly a single home left that was worth more than its mortgage, giving the term "underwater" new meaning. Thus, one did not have to wait for actual damage from higher seas to tell you to get out.

I have focused on homes, but nothing escaped the rising seas. They flooded roads, bridges, power plants, airports, ports, public buildings, office buildings, you name it. Compounding the problem was that as private and commercial property values dropped, so did the tax revenue that cities needed to operate and repair the flood damage, a weird kind of feedback. The result was that in Myrtle Beach and up and down the Atlantic Seaboard, a depression worse than anything seen in the 1930s took root. I say that because as miserable as people were during the Great Depression, there was at least a ray or two of hope. FDR had replaced Hoover and the New Deal was working, though not everyone benefited. People believed that if they just hung on, waited out the bad times, as a 1930s folk singer put it, "There's a better world that's a-coming." Then came WWII and the end of the Great Depression.

No one on the South Carolina coast back then, or anywhere, was singing about a better world a-coming. It wasn't and everyone knew it. For the first time in modern history, the hope of every parent that their children will have a better life than theirs was over. You may be going to talk with others about the effect this painful knowledge had on human psychology. It is one of the major facts of life in the late twenty-first century.

By about 2050, we knew that in deference to my father we had waited too long to sell Black House. The real estate market had collapsed, and Myrtle Beach was in the process of being abandoned by those who could leave, who were not trapped there by stubbornness or poverty or because they were elderly and infirm and had no one to help them move.

When he died in 2058, one hundred years after the first Black bought our family home, my sister and I just walked away and have never been back. The final insult, if you will, was that because the Ocean Woods Memorial Cemetery had been condemned due to high water, we could not bury our father in our family plot but had to inter him on higher ground inland, far from our old neighborhood.

You have indeed painted a painful picture of the fate of Myrtle Beach and other communities on the Atlantic Seaboard. From your scholarship, you know more than most about what happened in similar localities around the world. What has been their fate?

One of the things that I and other geographers noted was that the flight from the seacoasts happened gradually. The first to sell did not buy a mountain cabin atop the Great Smokies. No, they bought another beach home on higher ground a few miles inland, or where there was a high-enough bluff between the house and the high-tide line. But as the sea kept on rising, these second properties would then become endangered and eventually the owners would have to sell them and move again. No one wanted to do that twice, adding to the overall retreat.

As this happened on a global scale, one of the greatest migrations in human history began, with hundreds of millions moving inland. This is still going on and will go on for God knows how long—how long will the sea keep rising? No one knows how it will play out, for humanity has never seen a mass migration on a global scale before.

We geographers were among the first to call attention to the impending disaster of climate migration. Early in the century, a new academic specialty had appeared called "sea level rise scholarship." I have a pretty complete file on it and know it well. We scientists felt we had to start paying attention to this because so far, all the focus was on sea level rise as a coastal issue affecting only those communities—ones like my own Myrtle Beach. But it was obvious that the millions displaced by sea level rise would have to go elsewhere. We had an early example in the diaspora from New Orleans after Katrina, when her refugees wound up all over the country, but especially in Texas.

An earlier large-scale migration that could serve as a model came with the Dust Bowl, when an estimated 2.5 million left the dry Plains States, most headed for California. That had an enormous effect on both the places they left and the places they went to. Another example is the Great Migration, when 6 million African Americans left the rural South for the industrialized North. This caused the percentage of African Americans living in the South to fall from over 90 percent to about 50 percent over about forty years.

But these two migrations essentially took people from one part of the country to another. What did one scholar say? . . . Here it is: Under climate change people are going to go "from every coastal place in the U.S. to every other place in the U.S." He also predicted another ominous effect: Just as some people in New Orleans never left, just as many African Americans stayed in the South, so would many coastal residents refuse to leave and hang on no matter what. My dad is a pretty good example. Others wanted to leave but had no assets, nowhere to go, and no one to help them. They were trapped where they were and have created a huge burden for society.

When demographers in the 2020s tried to predict how many people might be displaced by rising seas, they used as a model those earlier migrations, when about 8.5 million people migrated out of a population of about 132 million Americans, or just over 6 percent. Global population was projected to reach close to 10 billion by 2050—of course, that projection ignored the fatal effects of global warming, but that was what people had to work with at the time. As I said earlier, about 50 percent of people around the world lived within 60 miles [100 km] of the seacoast, amounting to about 5 billion worldwide. If the same 6 percent as in 1930s America became climate refugees, that would have come to about 230 million worldwide just from sea level rise alone.

But keep in mind that many of the poor people of Oklahoma and other states, and the African Americans of the South, no doubt had good reason to migrate, but no one made them. They chose to move to have better lives, not to save their lives, so not surprisingly the 6 percent for climate migration has turned out to be quite low.

People have had to migrate not only because of sea level rise but also because of extreme heat, drought, famine, disease, desertification, water quality, and so on. No one knows how many people so far in this century have been forced or chose to migrate, but the number is in the billions worldwide.

Scholars today believe the number of migrants has peaked and is headed down, for two reasons: First, most who had the ability to migrate would have done so by now. Second, the number of places one can move safely to are dwindling. No one is going to find a community to welcome them. More likely they will be turned away at gunpoint.

Tavau Toafa is the last person alive to have been born in the foundered island nation of Tuvalu. I interviewed him thanks to the good offices of the Museum of New Zealand, Te Papa Tongarewa in Wellington, one of the few museums that has managed to keep its doors open.

Mr. Toafa, greetings. Please tell me how you come to be in New Zealand instead of your home island of Tuvalu.

If you could see me, you would certainly say that I look Polynesian, not like a typical Kiwi or Maori. I come not from here but from a place you can no longer find on any map, for it has disappeared beneath the waves. In the year the century was born, I was born too on the tiny atoll nation of Tuvalu. Look closely at one of the old atlases they have here at the museum, and you can find where Tuvalu used to be, just south of the equator and just west of the international date line. The first and till then the only time the outer world noticed Tuvalu was in World War II when General MacArthur built an airfield on one of our islands.

In 1978, Tuvalu gained its independence as a member of the British Commonwealth. By land area, Tuvalu was the fourth-smallest nation in the world, after the Vatican, Monaco, and Nauru. We had nine coral atolls, of 10 square miles [26 sq km] in total area, spread over 50,000 square miles [130,000 km] of the Pacific Ocean. When I was born in 2000, our population was only 9,420 people.

For centuries, we had lived by fishing and growing coconut, taro, and bananas. Then after the war we needed cash, which we earned by selling fishing licenses and our beautiful stamps to collectors around the world. Then with the coming of the Internet, Tuvalu was assigned the domain name dot tv. We made money selling the use of that name. It was rather like money falling from the sky.

Not long after you were born though, everything began to come apart for Tuvalu.

We burned almost no oil or coal; experts here at the museum say that Tuvalu emitted far less carbon dioxide than a small New Zealand town of the same population. But as the seas began to rise, Tuvalu's problem was geography. Our highest point was about 15 feet [4.5 meters] above sea level, and at my birth most of Tuvalu was less than 6.5 feet [2 meters] above sea level. If the sea kept on rising, we had no higher land to retreat to. When we learned that scientists were predicting the sea would rise by 3 feet [1 meter] or more, we knew that if they were right, Tuvalu was doomed.

I remember my parents telling me that by the time I was born, the regular moon cycle of high tides, combined with the higher seas, was making the ocean spill over onto our roads and fields and into our neighborhoods. Each year the sea seemed to reach a little farther and take a little longer to recede. My parents said that in the centers of the larger islands, seawater would squirt up through the coral bedrock and spill into the taro pits. The airport runway on Funafuti began to flood all the time, and that was our best way out in an emergency.

As the years went by, the warmer water bleached our coral reefs and they died, taking with them the fish that were our main source of protein. What little freshwater was available began to taste salty. Pacific cyclones seemed to have become stronger, and we knew that a really big one could wipe out our entire nation and leave our atolls uninhabitable.

When I was thirty, our government announced that we would have to abandon Tuvalu. By then, other Asian and Pacific nations had their own problems, so we did not know who would take us in. Several turned us away. But thanks be to God for the New Zealanders. To their everlasting credit, those Kiwis, of which I am proud to count myself one, welcomed us warmly. Their kindness allowed us to survive as individual persons and to maintain our Tuvalese culture. However, as our people intermarry, I fear that the day is coming when only historians will have heard of Tuvalu, and someday, no one.

Tuvalu was not the only island nation to founder. Kiribati, Tokelau, American Samoa, Tonga, and Guam sank beneath the waves or became so threatened that people abandoned them. And in the Indian Ocean too—the Seychelles, the Maldives, and Mauritius, for example. They tell me that the sea is going to keep on rising, so other island nations are sure to join them.

My grandfather was the last prime minister of the nation of Tuvalu. He made sure he was the last Tuvalese to depart our island. He told me that while walking up the ramp to board the ship leaving Tuvalu for New Zealand, holding our young flag to his chest, an overpowering sadness took hold of him. It was even more powerful than the sadness he felt when a family member or loved one died. Something larger than any individual or family was dying before his eyes, the very notion of what it meant to be Tuvalese. As our islands disappeared beyond the horizon, soon to sink beneath the waves, he knew he would never return and that our flag would never fly again. To have to abandon your homeland is one thing; people have had to do that throughout history. But to have it simply vanish is another. Then you know for sure that you and your children are never going back.

Monique van der Poll is the former Dutch minister of the environment. I spoke with her at her office in Maastricht.

We Dutch have a saying: "God created the world, but the Dutch made the Netherlands." With much of our land below sea level, before we could build cities we had to build barriers, dikes, and the polders that keep the sea out. We went on to become a leader in art, commerce, seafaring, and more. We always tried to be good world citizens. We dutifully cut our greenhouse gas emissions, but it made no difference. What did matter was what the *grote vervuilers*, the big polluters, America, China, and India, did. Back in 2000, the Netherlands emitted only one-half of 1 percent of global carbon dioxide. Even so, we cut those emissions by half, but on a global scale it was *"een druppel op een gloeiende plaat"*—a drop in the bucket, as you would say.

We Dutch had defied nature and the North Sea for centuries. When we have to retreat, the rest of the world had better look out. And retreat we have. I'm speaking with you from the seat of the Dutch government at Maastricht, the oldest city in the Netherlands. We moved the capital here in 2052 not because of the city's age and role in our history but because, at 161 feet [49 meters], Maastricht is our highest city and thus will be the last to flood.

Even our name, the Netherlands, told us that if sea level rose, we of the low-lying lands would be in trouble. We are. Much of Holland is under something all right, and that something is the North Sea. By the beginning of this century, more than two-thirds of our land was below sea level and two-thirds of us lived on that land. We fought the sea first with our windmills and then with electric pumps and marvelous engineering works like our great sea gates and barriers. Of course, we knew we played a dangerous game, but we believed that Dutch determination and ingenuity would give us a winning hand. We could not foresee that the rest of the world would rig the game against us.

Like people everywhere, we built our nation believing that the temperature, the rivers, the tides, sea level, and so on would behave as they always had. That allowed us to plan for the hundred-year flood, the five-hundred-year flood, *enzovoort*. "*Na regen komt zonneschijn*," we say—if it rains today, tomorrow the sun will shine. In other words, however bad things get, they will return to normal. But now the old normal is gone.

As the sea rose, Dutch land was also sinking, like delta land everywhere, which by itself causes sea level to rise relative to the land. Our worst problem historically, as you would expect, has been devastating floods. We had a big one in 1916 that caused us to spend a lot on flood protection. Then in January 1953 came an even bigger one that blasted through those protections to become famous in Dutch history. A high spring tide and 30 mile-per-hour [48 kph] winds raised a sea surge almost 20 feet [6 meters] above mean sea level and sent it crashing into our dikes. Many of them collapsed and nearly two thousand people and 30,000 animals died. We had to evacuate 70,000 people. Like a scene in one of our *sprookjes*—fairy tales—as the last dike was about to fail, the mayor of a town ordered a ship to sail into the hole in the dike and plug it like a giant finger, saving 3 million people from massive flooding. The scare from that flood launched us on a fifty-year program to strengthen our defenses against the North Sea.

At the end of the twentieth century, Rotterdam was the most active port in Europe and the backbone of the Dutch economy. It was our duty to protect Rotterdam at all costs. So, we started a new series of protections called the Delta Works, which included our grandest engineering achievement, the Maeslantkering, or storm surge barrier, at the mouth of the Rhine below Rotterdam. It was a pair of giant, curved sea gates, mounted on ball bearings 33 feet [10 meters] in diameter. Someone said it looked like two Eiffel Towers lying on their sides.

By the 1990s, dikes and barriers had sealed all the routes by which the North Sea could enter the Rhine delta at Rotterdam except one: a ship channel called the Nieuwe Waterweg. That channel was like your Mississippi River Gulf Outlet in New Orleans, a *kanaal* dug to give ships a faster route to the docks. But as you found out, such channels also provide a faster route inland for tidal and hurricane surges. The Maeslant gates were built to prevent water from traveling up the Nieuwe Waterweg to Rotterdam. We tested them in November 2007 and found that they performed perfectly. We believed they would protect us from the worst the North Sea could do, but that was twentieth-century thinking, and we were to face twenty-first-century problems that humanity had never encountered before.

Of course, we had long accepted the reality of global warming and did what we could to adapt. We knew the North Sea would keep rising. We even required our schoolchildren to learn to swim with their clothes and shoes on. Who else did that? At great expense, we had raised the height of the Maeslant gates from 72 to 82 feet [22 to 25 meters], but the sea just kept on rising. What were we supposed to do? Abandon our country to the sea? No Dutchman would do that.

By the middle of this century, although the gates had protected Rotterdam from several floods, the rising water had damaged the port facilities, which were a major source of income for Holland. We knew we ought to raise the height of the gates once again and were in the process of trying to figure out how to pay for it. Borrowing was out of the question because no bank or international fund would lend for such a project.

Then in January 2052, one year short of a century after the giant storm of 1953, a much larger storm raised a surge of North Sea water of 100 feet [30 meters], on top of the higher sea level, made effectively even higher by our land subsidence. Waves far taller than any Hollander had ever seen—and that is saying something—rolling in on those higher seas, crashed against the Maeslant gates and our other defenses against the sea. We closed the great southern barrier dam and the Maeslant gates and prayed. As the water rose higher, some surges began to overtop the gates. The right-hand gate facing inland began to wobble on its axis and then vibrate. The motion became more violent until the gate ripped off its foundation and fell into the channel. Now there was nothing to stop the North Sea and, like an arrow, the surge sped up the Nieuwe Waterweg and into the heart of Rotterdam. Within hours, all of Rotterdam was under 18 feet [5.5 meters], of water.

Believing that the Maeslant gates couldn't fail, the Rotterdam authorities had not evacuated the city. By the time they gave the order, many of the old and sick, who had no way to get out, drowned. Floodwaters trapped thousands in attics and prisoners in their cells; many others died trying to save their loved ones and pets.

No one will ever know the exact number who drowned in the great Rotterdam flood of 2052, because authorities never found thousands of the missing. Nevertheless, we estimate that one-third of Rotterdam's population of 800,000 people died in the storm and its aftermath, making it the greatest disaster in Dutch history.

To rebuild the Maeslant gates, restore Rotterdam's port facilities, and reconstruct the ruined city would have required far more money than we Dutch had at that time. Even if the government could have found the money, insurers, bankers, builders, and, most important, the people themselves had lost confidence in a coastal city like Rotterdam. The sea was going to keep rising and who could say that the next big storm would not be even larger? And that the one after that would not be larger still? I think we were the first nation to formally decide that our population would have to move inland, away from the coast. We Dutch mark January 31, 2052, the Fall of Rotterdam, as a national day of mourning. In March of that year, we moved the seat of the Dutch government here to Maastricht.

Because of the configuration of the coast and the way the storm waters approached, Amsterdam and other coastal cities survived the great storm of 2052 more or less intact. But there is no way to calculate the damage that Rotterdam's fall did to Amsterdam's self-image, confidence, and future. Rotterdam showed us how even the greatest works of Dutch engineering could not prevent the destruction of one of our major cities in a matter of hours. Amsterdam took years, not hours, to fail, but fail it did, a victim not of a great storm but of a great loss of confidence that the city could remain habitable in the face of future global warming, sea level rise, and storms. Perhaps that was the major lesson of Rotterdam: a loss of confidence in a city's future can be as deadly as any destructive force, man-made or natural.

The structures built to protect New York had failed in the storm of 2042. The Brits had built the Thames Barrier to prevent water from getting into the floodplain around London. It had been designed in the late 1970s and projected to last until 2030, but of course, the planners did not take into account global warming. It could have been modified to last longer, but by the 2020s Britain had become nearly paralyzed by internal divisions, and, being led by those who still denied global warming, did nothing. The Russians built a movable dam at St. Petersburg, your Army Corps of Engineers spent billions on what they already knew were inadequate defenses at New Orleans, other nations started their own projects, *enzovoort.* None have survived. It is impossible to build a barrier high enough to stop a sea that continues to rise higher each year, with no end in sight.

What happened to Dutch cities other than Rotterdam and Amsterdam?

Look at a map from the year 2000 and you can see which areas and cities were vulnerable. We have abandoned all those that were below sea level then, either because they flooded repeatedly or because we feared that one day they would flood. The Hague, Haarlem, Leiden, Delft, Harlingen, Groningen, and many other smaller cities and towns are gone now. We Dutch have had to give up our national strategy—perhaps even our national identity—and surrender back to the North Sea precious land we fought for centuries to win.

As of 2020, Holland had more than 17.5 million people living on about 16,000 square miles [41,500 sq km], for a population density of 420 people per square kilometer. That was the highest in Europe and just over one-third the population density of Bangladesh, which then had the highest density in the world. But as I mentioned earlier, half our land was below sea level; we have now had to abandon all that land, a fact that by itself doubled population density. But to make matters worse, by 2050 the population of the Netherlands had risen to 18 million; today, no one is sure what it is; let us say it remains 18 million. Those people live on half the land we had in 2020, so today's population density is about 870. And as we lose more land to the sea, unless our death rate increases further, which it well may, the number packed into a square kilometer is bound to increase.

You would have to be Dutch to know how much it pains me to say this, but our nation of mariners has become a nation of *landrots*—landlubbers, you say—squeezed into half of our land and tomorrow maybe into one-third. Our economy has collapsed, and reasonable people do not see how the Netherlands can survive as a nation. We have already made overtures to Germany and France about a merger. But I recall your English saying, "Equals do not merge." What assets do we Dutch have to bring to a union—a half-drowned country? We still have our Dutch identity and our pride, but how long could we retain them if we became part of Germany or France?

PART 4
ICE

César Garcia is Peru's minister of the environment. His family traces its roots to the time of Pizarro and Atahualpa. I interviewed Sr. Garcia at his home in Pucallpa, east of the Andes, where his family moved after the Fall of Lima.

Peru tends to be a land of extremes, especially in its topography and climate. If my ancestors had depended on rainfall alone for their water, they could never have survived on the arid, narrow, low-lying strip of earth between the Pacific coast and the Andes, for it is one of the driest places on the planet. The reason for this extreme aridity is that the western coast of South America lies in the rain shadow of the Andes. The cold Humboldt Current chills the moist Pacific air and as the air moves inland and rises, its moisture condenses as snow and falls on the Andean peaks. The process leaves Peru's coastal plain so dry that it receives only 2 percent of our country's precipitation. Yet at the turn of the century, the coast supported 70 percent of our population. How did we manage to support so many on so little? We Peruvians had our own *milagro de panes y los peces*.

Our greatest miracle may have been our capital, Lima. When this century began, Lima supported 7.3 million people on only 1 inch [25 mm] of rainfall each year—and most of that did not really fall as rain but drifted as a cool mist. Had Lima gathered every drop of moisture within its limits, the total would have come to 500 gallons [1,893 liters] per year for each resident. Compare that to the 200 gallons [757 liters] or more *per day* that the average person in one of your American desert cities used back then.

Obviously, Limeños had to get their water from somewhere other than the sky. And to maintain a great city, they had to be able to count on that water even in dry years. Fortunately, they had a dependable reservoir: the glaciers of the snowcapped peaks of the Cordillera Central. In winter the glaciers would build up; in summer they would send their meltwater down the Rimac River and into Lima. The next year, the same again. Those glaciers kept Lima alive. Without them, it would become a ghost city. As we say in another context, "*El que no trabaje que no coma.*" No mill, no meal. Or, in this context, no ice, no water. Those glaciers were our water factory.

All the Andean nations—Argentina, Bolivia, Chile, Colombia, Ecuador, Peru, and Venezuela—relied to some extent on melting glaciers for their water. La Paz and El Alto in Bolivia, for example, got most of theirs from the Chacaltaya glacier.

A few other parts of the world, such as East Africa and New Guinea, also once had tropical glaciers. Think of the great twentieth-century short story "Las Nieves del Kilimanjaro." But those countries had more rain than Peru and were not so dependent on the meltwater.

A glacier in the tropics is by definition *una contradicción frágil.* If the temperature goes up just a little, tropical glaciers begin to disappear. Even before this century, Andean glaciers had begun to melt rapidly. Between 1970 and 2000, Peru's glaciers shrank by nearly one-third. So did the glaciers on Cotopaxi in Ecuador. Back in 1983, a scientist predicted that Colombia's El Cocuy glaciers would last for at least three hundred years. A repeat study in 2005 lowered that to twenty-five years, and by the early 2030s the El Cocuy glaciers were gone.

Between 1980 and 2005, the glacier on one of our most famous peaks, 17,200-foot [5,250-meter] Pastoruri in our beautiful Huascarán National Park, shrank by 66 feet [20 meters] per year. By the end of that period, the glacier covered less than one square mile [1.6 sq km].

Within a decade, it too had disappeared. The Quelccaya ice cap in the Cordillera Oriental used to be one of the largest glaciers in the world, but by 2000 had receded more than a kilometer, and, by the middle of the century, it too had vanished.

Tropical glaciers in other parts of the world had also started to melt in the last century. Kilimanjaro had lost 75 to 85 percent of its ice and seven of Mt. Kenya's eighteen glaciers had disappeared. New Guinea's tropical glaciers were also shrinking. Today no tropical glaciers are left anywhere.

We Peruvians had plenty of warning, but we paid no heed. As the temperature went up, the glaciers of the Cordillera Central began to melt faster and send huge amounts of meltwater down our rivers. In the early decades of this century, our main concern was flooding, not drought. It was impossible to convince people and politicians that this was the feast before the coming famine—that someday the *milagro* would end. Our scientists said the change from too much water to too little would come during the early 2040s. They could not persuade our leaders to build reservoirs to store the high water and introduce strong conservation measures.

I suppose you could say that our Andean peaks had not been high enough. None in the Cordillera Central rise higher than 19,350 feet [6,000 meters] and, when the century began, their glaciers were all above 16,400 feet [5,000 meters]. The scientists told us that for each degree Celsius the temperature went up, the snow line at our latitude would rise about 490 feet [150 meters]. A fifth grader could do the arithmetic. If the average temperature in the high mountains rose by about 3 degrees—and scientists had told us that temperatures in the mountains rise more than in the plains—those glaciers were all bound to disappear. In our *negación*—denial—Limeños, like people everywhere, refused to accept the consequences of global warming until it was too late. When the glaciers had melted and the rivers had dried up, we had no reserves.

The poor were the first to feel the thirst. In the last century they had immigrated to Lima by the millions. By 2050, the city and Peru itself were depopulating, as the poor, carrying their few possessions on their backs or in carts, left the *barriades* and walked back to the highlands from which their ancestors had descended generations before. Most headed for the eastern side of the mountains, if they could get there, where enough rain still fell and from where I am speaking to you, señor. A seemingly endless human chain filled the roads leading from the coastal cities up to the mountain passes. Many fell by the wayside.

Another problem was that as the flow of the rivers fell, so did the amount of hydropower our dams generated. Hydropower once accounted for 80 percent of Peru's energy, and we had few fossil-fuel resources and no way to replace the missing hydropower. The lack of power was the main reason that, even though Peru had plenty of access to the sea, we could not use desalting.

As the cities became unlivable, the Maoist organization Sendero Luminoso, which had largely disappeared by the early years of the century, reemerged. It began to sponsor acts aimed at destabilizing the government, claiming with some accuracy that the wealthy were receiving secret water supplies at the expense of the poor. More and more of the poor joined Sendero Luminoso, as did thousands of defecting troops. Today, Peru has almost ceased to exist as a functioning state and has devolved into a set of armed camps, each protecting its local water supply.

Some South American countries and their corrupt leaders had sold water supplies and infrastructure to private foreign companies, supposedly capitalism at its best. But these companies were in business to make a profit. The moment that became impossible, the water companies simply walked away. In most cases, seeing what was coming, they had invested next to nothing in repair and maintenance, so that the equipment and facilities they left behind were useless to our crippled governments.

The most frightening thing about Peru's future is that we have enough water for only about one-third the number of people the country supported in 2000 and that water is at high altitudes or on the east side of the Andes. We need to abandon the coastal strip and build a new, high-elevation country on the eastern slope, but where do we get the resources, the leadership, the energy, the hope? How does a country simply abandon its largest cities and a large fraction of its territory and reestablish itself somewhere else? When in history has that ever happened? Yet, for some countries, that is what *el Calentamiento Grandes*, the Great Warming, means they must do if they hope to survive.

Today I speak with Yekaterina Zimova at her grandson's home in Vlad-ivostok. Born in the year 2000, Zimova is the daughter of Nikita Zimov and the granddaughter of Sergey Aphanasievich Zimov, a great Russian scientist and would-be habitat restorer during the first half of the century.

Katya Nikitovna, if I may so address you, tell me about yourself and your illustrious forefathers.

Я счастлив and with that I will go on in English. I used to speak it fluently when my father and grandfather worked with American and British scientists in the old days, but now I am out of practice. I will see how well I can do.

My grandfather Sergey Aphanasievich was in the first years of the century thought to be the top scientist in our country, one of the best in the world. This was not only because of his intellect but also because he studied permafrost, which would turn out not to be so permanent and which contributed far more to глобальное потепление, your global warming, than other scientists had predicted.

In 1977, Sergey Aphanasievich helped establish the Northeast Science Station in Cherskii as a research institute of the Russian Academy. This small Siberian town where I was born lies at 69° North, above the Arctic Circle, at the mouth of the Kolyma River about 93 miles [150 km] south of the Arctic Ocean. The mission of the center was to study the permafrost, the methane gas it gave off, and its effect on the ecosystem. But before I go into that I need to tell you about another project for which he really became famous, the Pleistocene Park.

My grandfather and father wanted to solve one of the biggest mysteries of science: what caused the woolly mammoth and the other large plant-eaters to disappear at the end of the last ice age? Most Siberian scientists thought the climate had warmed up and changed grasslands to tundra—it is the same word in both our languages—which did not provide enough food to keep the big animals alive. My granddad thought this was just backward, that the trampling and manure from large herds would have turned the tundra into grassland. That would have left human hunters as the only way to explain the extinction. But if the extinction was due to overhunting and not climate change, it might be possible to reestablish large mammals on the tundra. The effort to do so became known as Pleistocene Park. My grandfather established a wildlife preserve and tried to stock it with wild bison, moose, elk, and so on, captured alive or bought as calves. When he died, my father carried on the work.

But it was the other line of research, the permafrost studies, that turned out to be the most important.

Yes, it was. Of course, I was brought up with scientists and even though I did not become one, I can explain about permafrost. They say it occurs when the temperature of the top of the ground is at or below freezing for at least two years. This turns the ground hard enough to build on and also keeps the frozen vegetation from being eaten by bacteria, and one gram of frozen soil can contain millions of bacteria. When the temperature rises and the permafrost thaws out, those millions come back to life and begin to eat the plants. But when they do that, they release both CO_2 and methane—coal gas we used to call it. These are the gases of the greenhouse and, tragically, CO_2 lasts much longer in the atmosphere than methane, but by the molecule, methane is twenty times as heat producing. I used to hear them talking about how this led to what they called a feedback, a Обратная связь we say.

How did that work?

Okay. Say that global warming raises the temperature above the permafrost. That causes the vegetation to rot and decay and be eaten by the now lively bacteria, which gives off CO_2 and methane, which goes into the atmosphere, which raises global temperature—and there is your feedback. If there was nothing else going on, it would continue until all the permafrost was gone. That may be where we are headed and if it happens, global warming will be more severe and last longer than even the worst predictions scientists have made.

I remember when I was a girl hearing my father talk about how the thawing permafrost was already obvious in Cherskii, where houses were sinking and some tilting over and falling on their sides. When people tried to rebuild, they could get through the now-warm layer at the top, but several inches farther down the ground was still hard as a rock and you couldn't drill into it to sink a piling.

Today, Cherskii has long been abandoned. The largest city situated entirely on permafrost was Yakutsk, which was about 280 miles [450 km] south of the Arctic Circle. We used to go there in my childhood to see what a big city offered. It had about 250,000 people then. Now it too is abandoned. If you went around the world looking at cities close to the Arctic Circle built all or partly on permafrost, you would find nearly all of them either vacant or soon to be. In Russia and Scandinavia, that would be not only Cherskii and Yakutsk but also Murmansk, Archangel, Norilsk, Tromsø, and many smaller ones. In the other hemisphere, Fairbanks, Echo Bay, and Yellowknife.

The computer models of the climate had projected that the Arctic would warm twice as fast and reach temperatures twice as high as in the rest of the world, and they were right. The models showed that once the permafrost started to thaw, feedbacks would keep it thawing.

Anyone living within a few hundred miles of the Arctic Circle knows their property is doomed, if not in this century, then in the next.

My father left behind all the scientific papers he had collected, his own and others, and marked a few for special attention if anyone wanted to look back and see how previous generations had made sure to destroy our world—their grandchildren's world, you could say. In preparing for our conversation, I looked at some of those, which made painful reading I can tell you.

One report from 2018 was written by a group of mainly Finnish geologists, whose country extended above the Arctic Circle and who needed to know the effect global warming would have on permafrost. They said that by 2050—only thirty-two years in the future for them and thus likely during the lifetimes of most of the people reading the paper—four million people and about three-fourths of the инфраструктура—infrastructure—would be exposed to permafrost damage. This turned out to be accurate, but of course, we are now thirty-four years beyond that point with no end to permafrost thawing in sight.

I found another paper that accurately predicted that the melting permafrost would shut down oil and gas operations in Alaska, including the oil wells on the North Slope and the Trans-Alaska and other pipelines. Also, the area in northwest Siberia where the main EU gas pipeline begins. One has to laugh—it is better than crying, no?—that the fossil-fuel companies became their own victims. Of course, they are gone everywhere now, but I can imagine my father giving his ironic smile over that prediction in this paper. This is maybe why he marked it.

What last thoughts do you have for my readers?

I am proud of my father and grandfather for what they tried to do for humanity. The sad thing is that the so-called leaders of those days could not tell the difference between the Pleistocene Park—a scientific dream probably doomed to fail—and the rock-hard science of man-made global warming about which nearly every scientist in the world agreed. I'm not sure we Russians, who have known great tyrants and despots, even have words to label those who destroyed our world, but let this grandmother try: *Убийцы нерожденных детей*—murderers of children unborn.

Marie Pungowiyi is a native Alaskan Eskimo and an anthropologist. She visited my home during a trip to the lower forty-eight.

No one knows when the Eskimo people first arrived on the island of Kigiktaq, where my people come from, but archaeologists have found evidence that we were there hundreds of years before the white man arrived. The island had a protected harbor, but the shore of the Chukchi Sea is an unforgiving place, especially when there is nothing to block the wind. We made our living from the sea, but the Chukchi could turn on you in fifteen minutes. My people and a lot of other western Alaskans almost died out in the 1880s, a time we call the Great Famine, after Yankee whalers killed all our walrus and whales. Around 1900, our village grew up as a supply depot for gold miners. Then in 1997, even before sea level got so high, one big storm eroded 33 feet [10 meters] of the north shore of our village, forcing us to relocate some homes and buildings.

Of course, such storms had always occurred, but we Kigiktaq Eskimos had survived them and the worst that the Bering Strait and the Chukchi Sea could throw at us. Early in this century, that began to change. Back then my great-great uncle, Caleb Pungowiyi, was special advisor on Native Affairs to the Marine Mammal Commission. I'd like to read to you from a report he wrote at that time:

> Our ancestors taught us that the Arctic environment is not constant, and that some years are harder than others. But they also taught us

that hard years are followed by times of greater abundance and cel-
ebration. As we have found with other aspects of our culture's an-
cestral wisdom, modern changes, not of our doing, make us wonder
when the good years will return.

As my ancestor feared, the good years did not return. My people had to abandon Kigiktaq entirely and relocate. Then larger storms
than our people had ever known destroyed the village, leaving the land
the way the first Eskimos must have found it when they crossed the
Bering Strait thousands of years ago. The same thing has happened
across the Arctic: Native peoples have been unable to maintain their
traditional survival strategies in today's warmer world and have had to
abandon their homes and villages.

I know that before global warming really got going, people claimed
it would benefit Arctic people. All that troublesome ice would melt,
and we would enjoy the warmer temperatures. How ignorant can you
get? Didn't they know that many of our towns were built on permafrost? As it thawed, it was like having the solid ground melt away beneath you. That even affected our cities: The ground in Fairbanks got
so unstable that the city had to abandon many buildings.

My great-great uncle's report shows just how much conditions
had changed on Kigiktaq even by the first decade of this century. As
temperatures warmed—and remember, they warmed twice as much
in the Arctic as they did globally—more sea ice melted and earlier
each year, moving the ice pack farther offshore. Walruses, seals, and
polar bears went with the ice and often wound up too far away for us
to hunt—and too far for the animals to get back to solid ice or land, so
many of them died.

When the sea, the wind, and the temperature changed, the animals needed to change too, but they did not know how. *Nuna-*

vak—walrus—has to haul out on the ice and rest between feedings; otherwise they just wear out. But as the ice melted and their resting places got farther from where they fed, the walruses had to waste too much energy getting back to the ice. They lost weight, and more and more of them died. The melting ice affected the basking seals—*otok*—the same way. As the ice melted earlier, the seals had to abandon their ice dens before their pups were old enough to survive. The poor little creatures just died before they could even get started.

Everywhere polar bears once lived they have now disappeared. Walruses and bears are not fish; they cannot swim forever. Bears also have to haul out to rest, mate, and rear their young. To do those things, they must have ice. The more the ice melted, the farther the bears had to swim to get to it, the more energy they spent, and the lower their chances of surviving. Scientists were not even sure how such isolated, solitary creatures as the polar bear ever found a mate, but, however they did it, the less ice, the harder it was. Bear dens that melted too early altered hibernation patterns and forced cubs out before they had grown large enough to survive, just like the seals. In some areas up here, as the sea ice melted the bears moved closer to towns, where our native hunters and those sickening trophy seekers could shoot them. That slowed down for a while after the U.S. government listed the polar bear as endangered in 2008, but it soon resumed when the government failed to enforce the regulation. A name on a list is meaningless unless the law is enforced.

One of the saddest things my people encountered was bears swimming far from land or ice—sometimes our hunters found them dozens of miles from either. You see, the bears did not have a map or a computer. They did not know that if they kept swimming they would eventually get beyond the point of no return. They did not know that the ice that had always been there for them was now gone. We first came across them swimming; then we found their floating carcasses. If they had not been dead for too long, our hunters towed them back for meat and pelts. But after a while we never even saw dead bears. The last *nanuk* was seen in the wild in 2031. The bears do breed in captivity, so people can see *nanuk* in zoos, which still have a few. Count me out on that. Anyway, the zoos are about finished too.

As the polar bear has gone, so I fear my people must go. Our traditional ways of life have melted away with the ice, and there has been nothing to replace them. We have no industry, no jobs, and without hunting, no way of sustaining ourselves, isolated up here as we are. Sure, it's warmer—but that has hurt us, not helped us. What will people do with the last Eskimo—put her in a zoo?

PART 5
WAR

General Moshe Eban retired from the Israeli army in 2070. He is an authority on the war of 2038, known as the Four-Day War, in which he served as a young artillery officer in the Golan Heights.

General Eban, this century has proved that in a dry land, the man upstream is king.

Yes, and that fact caused every nation in the region to try to hold the high ground. Israel knew that while religion, nationalism, and history were sources of conflict between us and the Arab nations, the ultimate fight would be over water—the one thing no nation and no person can do without. When Egyptian president Anwar Sadat signed a peace treaty with Israel more than a century ago—and sealed his doom—he said that if Egypt ever went to war again, it would be to protect its water resources. In 1990, King Hussein said that water was the only reason Jordan would go to war with Israel. Ban Ki-Moon, a secretary-general of the UN before the organization collapsed, warned that a lack of water was going to lead to twenty-first-century wars. And the events of this century have proved each of them right. The leaders of Israel did not need to make such statements—it was obvious that without water our experiment in nation building was bound to fail.

Ever since Israel declared itself an independent state, she fought over water with her Arab neighbors—everything from skirmishes to full-out wars. The root of the problem can be traced all the way back to the 1948 Arab–Israeli war. It ended in an armistice, but by failing to specify how the countries of the Jordan basin would divide the available river water, the agreement made future conflicts unavoidable. Without such specificity, Israel and the other countries of the basin had no choice but to begin taking the water they needed. To prevent Israel from having access to the Jordan River, the neighboring Arab countries announced that they planned to divert its headwaters in the Golan. That would deny most of Israel the waters of the Jordan and the Yarmouk River. We could not allow that and so in 1967 launched what became known as the Six-Day War. During that brief conflict, Israel took the Golan Heights, where I later served, blocking the Arab plans and gaining control of the upper Jordan. Israel also got half the length of the Yarmouk, compared with the 6 miles [10 km] we had controlled before the war. After the Six-Day War, when Jordan wished to develop its section of the Yarmouk, it had to get our consent.

Water also played a prominent role in the evolution of the old Palestinian Liberation Organization. When the PLO emerged with new leadership after the Six-Day War, it began to raid Israeli settlements in the Jordan Valley, including pumping stations and other water installations. In retaliation, Israel attacked Jordan's East Ghor Canal and put it out of business. We then struck a secret deal that allowed Jordan to repair the canal, but in return it had to expel the PLO. That led to fighting between the Jordanians and the PLO in a time known as Black September. That battle sowed lasting hatreds in a part of the world where memories are long. Even though these events happened in the last century, they are key to understanding the origins of the twenty-first-century conflict in the Middle East.

The region suffered a serious drought in the early years of this century. As global warming raised temperatures and lowered rainfall, river flows continued to decline. By 2030, the Jordan had shrunk by 20 percent, requiring Israel and its neighbors to pump more from underground aquifers. But groundwater is fossil water that took thousands of years to accumulate. We were depleting the groundwater far faster than nature could replenish the aquifers. As populations grew and we pumped out more, water tables dropped further and further. We could see the time was coming when the water level would be so deep that even our strongest pumps could not lift it. Remember, water is heavy: one cubic foot weighs 62 pounds [28 kg]. To get it from the depth to the surface takes a huge amount of energy.

The root problem was plain even in the first decade of this century, when even before global warming began to lower the Jordan's discharge, more water had been promised to Israel, Jordan, and Syria than the river held. I understand that in your country in the old days you called that "paper water."

Growing populations made everything worse. In 2000, 2.9 million Palestinians lived in the West Bank and Gaza. By 2015, the number had grown to about 4.5 million, and by 2030, to 6 million. Israel had similar population increases. Thus, by the mid-2020s, there were many more Palestinians and Israelis, but, because of global warming, even less water than there had been.

By the 2020s, organizations like Hamas and Hezbollah, funded by Iran, were flush with cash. Attacks on Israel increased steadily and we found ourselves powerless to stop them. That's because Israel was no longer the only Middle Eastern state to have nuclear weapons. Iran had left the nuclear nonproliferation group and conducted several underground tests, so there was no longer any doubt that when, back in the first decade, she had claimed to be building nuclear facilities for peaceful purposes, Iran was actually building bombs. Israel had once bombed and destroyed an Iranian nuclear reactor, but that only caused the Iranians to bury their facilities so deep that any nuclear strike on them would produce a huge cloud of fallout that could then drift in any direction, including back on Israel. By the late twenties, we knew that the Iranians had a stockpile containing at least several dozen nuclear warheads—and it would take only a handful to obliterate Israel. We feared that some of the organizations whose announced policy was to "wipe Israel off the map" had also acquired nuclear weapons in the global atomic bazaar that had grown up by then.

Thus, for the first time since the founding of Israel in 1948, we Israelis began to lose confidence in our nation's survival. As we always did when we were in trouble, we appealed to our patron, the United States. In a secret summit between our leaders and yours in Malta in 2028, we had received assurance that if Israel had to go to war, America would take all necessary steps, including the use of tactical nuclear weapons, to defend us. But if there is one thing that we in the Middle East have learned, it is that promises are made to be broken. Would America keep its word?

In 2038, Egypt began to mass troops along the Negev border, as it had done several times in the twentieth century. At 6 P.M. on October 15 of that year, just at sunset when the sun was in our eyes, Egyptian tanks followed by two regiments of troops crossed the border into the Negev. We responded with armor, troops, and planes and halted the Egyptians in their tracks. We had checkmated them, but it seemed too easy. Some of our generals suspected a feint.

To control water supply in the Jordan basin, as the old saying goes, get upstream—occupy the Golan Heights. That has been the rule since ancient times. In the Six-Day War, that is just what Israel had done, giving us control over both the upper Jordan and the Yarmouk. Two days after the Egyptian incursion, Syria, Jordan, and Syria's client state Lebanon launched a coordinated, full-out, three-pronged attack in the Golan that caught our military by surprise. Looking back, I can see that spending ninety years surrounded by enemies dedicated to wiping Israel out had worn us down. How long can a country stay in a perpetual state of alert? With so many well-armed enemies, and three of them attacking us in the Golan, we feared that, if we fought a conventional war, Israel could well lose. Our only option was to threaten to use our atomic weapons.

We sent diplomats under white flags to Amman, Beirut, Cairo, and Damascus. We informed those governments that, as they had long known, Israel had atomic weapons and that they were armed and loaded on our supersonic Aurora stealth fighter-bombers, obtained from the United States, and targeted at the four capitals. Our enemies knew that, flying at Mach 6, some if not all the Auroras would escape radar detection and reach their targets. Even if enemy radar did detect them, they traveled at 4,000 miles per hour [6,440 kph], so that the 250-mile [400-km] flight from Tel Aviv to Cairo would take less than ten minutes, allowing for slower takeoff speeds, making it impossible for the enemy planes to shoot down every Aurora.

Then Iran made its move, announcing that, in anticipation of a request from its Arab brothers, it had already sent part of its nuclear arsenal to Syria, following up with a massive transfer of troops to join the fight to obliterate the nation of Israel, a longtime goal of Iran. Remember that by this time the United Nations and its International Atomic Energy Agency were both long defunct, leaving Israel with no choice but to face alone what would likely seal its fate: that we were not the only Mideast power to have nuclear weapons. If we used ours, the Arabs would use theirs and the entire region might go up in an atomic conflagration.

Our only option was to appeal to the United States to live up to its promise and enter the Golan war on our side. You had more nuclear weapons than any country and better means to deliver them. U.S. warships loaded with nuclear-armed cruise missiles were already sailing the eastern Mediterranean. You could have destroyed those four capitals with impunity.

But you were preoccupied with your own problems and ignored our hotline calls. As the hours ticked by with no response, and with a steady loss of ground in the Golan, we realized the game was up. We had no choice but to sue for peace and agree to withdraw to the Green Line and the land that Israel occupied immediately after the 1948 Arab–Israeli War. We had to give up the Golan, the West Bank, the Gaza Strip, and formally recognize the State of Palestine. Now to get water, we had to appeal to the Palestinians, our longtime enemies. Events had reversed our roles; now we Israelis were the oppressed, desperate, and thirsty minority. Our defeat took four days; hence our enemies derisively call it the Four-Day War.

Of course, the outcome satisfied no one. Israel had lost everything she had gained between 1948 and 2038. Our leaders feared that, having won so much, our enemies would want even more and would push Israel into the sea. But then a curious thing happened.

As the effects of global warming grew worse, as global oil production declined, Arab states had too much on their minds to obsess about Israel. The despotic petrostates and their patrons could see the handwriting on the wall, and it spelled out their obituary. The Palestinians had won the land and statehood they had long desired, so they and their supporters quieted down. We laid low, as you Americans say, and after a while reached a strange kind of détente with our Arab neighbors. Maybe the more effort people have to spend just to survive, the less they have for hatred and war.

What the future holds we cannot know. One thing we do know is that as the world continues to warm and our region gets even drier, there will not be enough water to sustain the present Middle East population. As in many parts of the world, the question is how we get from today's population down to a sustainable one.

Field Marshall Raj Manekshaw is chief of the Indian Army, headquartered at the capital of Hyderabad. At the time of the 2050 Indus War between India and Pakistan, General Manekshaw was a young lieutenant serving in the Rann of Kutch.

I have read that at the beginning of the century, some said it was absurd to believe that global warming could lead to war, much less to the use of atomic weapons. Those people surely knew nothing of the history of India and Pakistan! Three times already in the twentieth century we fought, and three times India won. Pakistan and Bangladesh were born in war. As the Pakistanis themselves say, "*Naa adataan jaandiyan ne, Bhavein katiye pora pora ji*"—A man never abandons his habits, even if he is cut to pieces. We had fought over land and national pride—did they think we would not fight over something as precious as water?

Remember that India takes its very name from a river: the Indus. It rises in the meltwater from the glaciers of the Karakoram mountain range—once they covered 7,000 square miles [18,000 sq km]—and flows mainly west through our territory of Jammu and Kashmir, then through the Punjab and across most of Pakistan to enter the Indian Ocean at Karachi. The word "punjab" means five rivers, the five main tributaries of the Indus. The great river turns the Punjab into Pakistan's breadbasket and supplies almost all of its potable water. Whoever controls the Indus controls the Punjab, and we knew that one day we would have to settle who did. Global warming brought that day upon us.

Being downstream from Indian territory, the Pakistanis rightly feared that India might one day dam the upper Indus and its tributaries and, when war came, shut off the water supply to Pakistan. Or, as has happened in other wars, release the water from reservoirs and flood everything downstream.

In order to ease these fears, in 1960 the two countries signed the Indus Waters Treaty. It gave India control over the easternmost rivers of the Punjab and Pakistan control over the westernmost ones. Peace broke down over the rebirth of East Pakistan as Bangladesh and led to the Indo–Pakistani War of 1971. It did not take long for dams and hydroelectric projects to become targets of the war. On December 5, 1971, Indian Hunter aircraft attacked and damaged the Mangla Dam in Pakistan, one of the world's largest at the time. By then we had already defeated the Pakistan Air Force and the skies above the Punjab were ours. For better or worse, we did not revoke the water treaty in any of our three wars with Pakistan.

By the middle of this century, India and Pakistan each had hundreds of plutonium bombs and the missiles to deliver them. We Indians estimated that we had enough weapons, many with multiple warheads, to obliterate every Pakistani city of more than 500,000 people several times over. But, we knew, so did the Pakistanis. Both countries also knew that, given the history of enmity between us, it would not take much to trigger another war. And by the middle of the century, the issue that would start the twenty-first-century Indo–Pakistani War was already evident: not territory, not religion, but water. The Indus, which had been our namesake and our blessing, now became the curse that launched the Indian subcontinent into nuclear war.

As the global climate warmed up during the first few decades of this century, the Karakoram glaciers on which the Indus and the other rivers of Jammu and Kashmir and the Punjab depended melted rapidly. For two decades, they flowed higher than at any time since re-cord-keeping began in the 1800s. The devastating floods that resulted made it hard to get anyone to listen to the scientists, who were telling us that once the glaciers had largely melted, instead of floods the Pun-jab would have drought.

By the late 2040s, runoff in the Indus had fallen by 30 percent. Jammu and Kashmir and the Punjab faced the same prospect that had devastated Bangladesh: that the rivers on which each depended would run dry for several months each year, causing massive crop failures and famine that threatened the very survival of the Punjab and Paki-stan.

Foreseeing these shortages, we began to construct new storage dams in Jammu and Kashmir, upstream from the Punjab. We also raised the height of existing dams so their reservoirs would hold more water. With hindsight, we can see these were foolish projects, for to fill new or heightened reservoirs requires surplus water and there was none. But people could not break out of the old belief that the way to solve a water shortage is to build new dams. In an attempt to fill our reservoirs we cut water flows to Pakistan, even though that meant the dams would generate less electrical power for us. But, we had learned, a nation can live with less electricity but not without water.

In an earlier time, Pakistan would have protested India's actions to the United Nations and asked its on-and-off-again patron, the United States, to intervene and persuade us to release more water. But the UN was no longer around and the only avenue for Pakistan was to appeal directly to India and ask us to revise the Indus Waters Treaty. Again, in an earlier time, we might have acceded. By the 2040s, no nation would voluntarily give up water over which it had control—note that I say control, not "legal right." We were upstream and in control of the water. India spurned the Pakistani request to renegotiate the treaty and continued to impound water on the Indus and its tributaries in Jammu and Kashmir.

Looking back, I believe that, in this general climate of distrust and antagonism, two events in particular triggered the twenty-first-century Indo–Pakistani War. Ever since partition in 1947, insurgents had conducted attacks and sabotage in Jammu and Kashmir; sometimes in India itself. In the 2040s, as the water supply began to drop and Pakistan had an increasing interest in gaining control of Jammu and Kashmir, those attacks escalated. They rose to a new and dangerous level when Pakistani commandos and insurgents bombed and partially destroyed the Salal Dam and power station on the Chenab River in Indian territory in the Vale of Kashmir. This had the immediate effect of releasing floodwaters downstream. That damaged both countries, but, after the floodwaters receded, the Chenab resumed its unimpeded flow down to Pakistan, leaving them better off than before the attack. We regarded this strike as tantamount to war.

Second, in May 2048, with water shortages full upon us, Pakistani guerrillas bombed our parliament building, killing several dozen members of the government. The prime minister escaped only because he had left through a rear exit a few minutes before the blast.

We captured two of the bombers and, although they carried no papers, our skilled interrogators got them to confess that they were Pakistani. Believe me, you do not want me to describe those skills. The Pakistani government denied any knowledge of the attacks, but of course they would. We demanded that Pakistan close all of its rebel camps in Jammu and Kashmir and cede to India a border strip 31 miles [50 km] wide so we could prevent new insurgents from infiltrating. When the Pakistanis refused, we closed the valves on all our dams upstream from their border, cutting off their water supplies in the Punjab.

We military men knew that war, likely nuclear, could not be avoided. We began to arm our nuclear weapons and load them onto our missiles and knew that the Pakistanis were doing the same. An Indian commando team crossed the Line of Control in Mendhar and seized the Mangla Dam on the Jhelum River just inside Pakistani territory, the same dam we had attacked in 1971.

The Pakistanis warned that, unless the Indian troops immediately withdrew and left the Mangla Dam undamaged, they would act and that all options would be on the table. If we had any trouble understanding what they meant, the president of Pakistan in unusually blunt language reminded India and the world that his country had never renounced the use of nuclear weapons in war nor precluded a first strike.

On April 14, 2050, Pakistan detonated a tactical fission bomb that completely wiped out an Indian battalion stationed near the Mangla Dam—my battalion. I had been away meeting with our generals and was on my way back to my men. Otherwise, I would have perished with them. For me, that made it personal. The weapon was triggered to go off in the air, which meant that although everyone below died instantly, there was none of the fallout that a ground blast would have caused. Perhaps it was a sign of Pakistani restraint that they used only a 5-kiloton tactical weapon and triggered it in the air. If so, the strategy failed to produce a similar restraint on our side.

Our response was to drop a 200-kiloton plutonium bomb on Lahore, ignited on impact. It obliterated the city and caused an estimated 1 million deaths. We followed up with a demand that Pakistan cease using nuclear weapons and enter into peace negotiations. But we have a saying in Hindi, *"Bhains ke aage been bajana"*—playing the flute to a buffalo is a waste. Sadly, the 100-year enmity between our two countries led Pakistani leaders to turn down India's proposal. At the moment they announced that they were refusing our offer, two dozen Pakistani missiles armed with plutonium devices ranging up to 300 kilotons were already in the air. Dozens of multiple independently targetable reentry vehicles (MIRVs) struck Bangalore, Calcutta, and New Delhi, completely destroying all three. The attack obliterated the seat of the Indian government and everything for miles around, but, of course, we had secretly moved our government and military leaders here to Hyderabad. The Pakistanis did not bother bombing Mumbai, our largest city, for sea level rise and monsoon rains had already flooded half of it, killing tens of thousands and leaving hundreds of thousands—maybe millions—homeless. Mumbai's train stations, stock exchange, and most important public buildings were already in ruins. I suppose our enemies decided not to waste a perfectly good bomb on a city that was doomed anyway.

Our early warning systems had been on high alert for weeks and had no trouble detecting the heat signature of the Pakistani missiles within seconds of their launch. Before a single one had landed, ours were on the way. The Pakistanis had boasted that the United States had provided them with a foolproof missile defense system, but our intelligence had revealed that neither the United States nor Pakistan had a system that worked, if either had ever worked, which we doubted. We had more and larger warheads and more-accurate missiles to deliver them. India could have ended all life in Pakistan if it chose and still have enough of its own population alive to carry on. We knew it and they knew it.

After our warheads destroyed Islamabad and Karachi, our leaders paused the attack but announced the list of remaining targets. It included every city in Pakistan, all its dams, military installations, nuclear-weapons labs, and the like. We reminded our enemies of a Hindu saying: "Many dogs kill a hare, no matter how many turns it makes."

Our prime minister announced to the press that, if necessary, we were prepared to return Pakistan to the Stone Age. One item on the target list was particularly influential: the site of the secret mountain bunker to which the Pakistani government had retreated but that our spies had located. We announced that we had reserved the largest hydrogen bomb ever exploded—a true bunker-busting penetrator—for that site and that it sat armed atop a fueled missile, with our finger on the button. We gave them twenty-four hours to respond.

Both countries had run countless simulations of nuclear war. They showed that a continuation of the war would destroy both countries and leave no winner. By this time, with scores of millions killed in a few hours, whatever lust for revenge either side felt had been sated. We were truly facing the abyss. Our president quoted the Bhagavad Gita: "If the radiance of a thousand suns were to burst at once into the sky, that would be like the splendor of the Mighty One. Now I am become Death, the destroyer of worlds." He told us he did not want to be the one to fulfill that prophecy.

A faction of the Pakistani government, supported by the army, then launched a coup that overthrew their leadership and established a new group in power, leaders who were willing to step back from the precipice. Both sides had set up a satellite phone hotline directly into the bunkers of the other. Within hours of the destruction of Islamabad and Karachi, the leaders of the two countries had negotiated a cease-fire.

One result of our fourth victory over Pakistan was that India acquired sovereignty over Jammu and Kashmir, and the southern half of the Punjab. But without adequate water, these provinces have proven to be more of a burden than a boon. Thus, the war accomplished little other than the death of vast numbers of Indians and Pakistanis. By now, with the Punjab too hot and dry for wheat and with Pakistan having lost three major cities, it is hard to see a future for that country, which was born in war and may have died in war.

How many people do you judge died in the war?

We can estimate fairly accurately how many died in Indian and Pakistani cities as a direct result of the ground blasts. We know how many succumbed to radiation poisoning in the first few weeks that followed the war. Now, some thirty-four years later, we can estimate how many eventually died from cancer and other illnesses that we can reasonably attribute to the widespread radiation that fell over both countries. The most plausible estimate I have seen is that the fourth Indo–Pakistani War cost 150 million lives.

The Honorable Neale Fraser was the first governor of the American state of Manitoba. I spoke to him from his residential care home in the state capital, Winnipeg.

Many of my fellow Canadians consider me a quisling—a collaborator at best, a traitor at worst. That is an easy judgment for them to make, because they did not have the responsibility I did. Canada had lost the war, further resistance would get us nowhere, or worse, and as the premier of Manitoba, my job was to make the best of a bad situation on behalf of the province and Canada. Moreover, I was under orders from Ottawa and Prime Minister Pierre Campbell. Had I refused to assume office as governor of the American state of Manitoba, I would have been relieved instantly and someone less committed would have been handed the job. So, I believe that history has vindicated me and restored my reputation. At least my conscience is clear.

Of course, I regret the loss of the sovereign nation of Canada as much as anyone. But we here in Manitoba are still far better off than 99 percent of the people in the world. We have a favorable climate, enough to eat, and are as self-sufficient as any people could be, growing and making everything we need right here. We are living the way our ancestors did in the early nineteenth century and they did fine. Plus, and the importance of this cannot be overestimated, being located in the center of a continent without, at least for the first few decades of the century, hordes of climate refugees massing at your border is not just an advantage but key to survival as a nation. But of course, we did have neighbors across a border, and therein hangs our tale.

It should not have come as a surprise to anyone on either side of the border that if global warming got bad enough, America would invade Canada. As it got hotter in the lower tier of your American states, there was an exodus from places like Houston and Phoenix and many of those people moved to the tier of states just below our border. From there they could look north and see our wide-open spaces, cooler climate, and amber fields of grain.

Not only were temperatures in the midsection of America becoming uncomfortable for people, they became increasingly unfavorable for wheat. Agronomists had projected that a rise in temperature of 2°F [1.1°C] would cause wheat yields to decrease by somewhere between 5 and 15 percent, and the total temperature rise by now has been three times that. Already by the 2040s, the red winter wheat on which Texas and Oklahoma had depended could no longer be grown there. It was still possible to raise red winter wheat in Colorado and Kansas, but you couldn't make a profit. The red spring wheat that had once flourished in your northern states like Montana, the Dakotas, and Minnesota could no longer be grown there at all: the climate that favored that type of wheat had migrated up here. American farmers knew it was only going to get hotter, making it harder and eventually impossible to grow the type of wheat they had always grown. Any American wheat farmer paying attention could see that his children, if they could be persuaded to try farming, would either have to grow a different kind of wheat or give up. During the second half of the twenty-first century, North American wheat farming was going to take place in Canada, not in the U.S. And at some point, people the world over began to realize that global warming was not going to stop anytime soon, so that if things were bad in some way today, tomorrow they would be worse. In other words, even if your American children could still farm wheat, odds were their children would not be able to.

As temperatures rose and crops failed, more and more Americans wanted to emigrate up here. In the 2030s, as the pressure for immigration began to build, we closed the border and ended legal immigration into Canada, as you had done with your southern neighbors.

But we could not end illegal immigration. The U.S.-Canada border was the longest undefended international boundary in the world: 3,145 miles [5,060 km] on land and 2,380 miles [3,830 km] on water. There was no way to prevent thousands of Americans from crossing into Canada each year illegally, just as thousands of Mexicans had once crossed your southern border.

After the sunbirds, as we called them, got across the border, they had no trouble finding camps of fellow Americans who would take them in. These camps soon became tinderboxes of anti-Canadian sentiment, and many of them were well armed. You Americans had the highest rate of gun ownership of any country and your guns emigrated with you. We were about to learn just how well armed you were.

Morris, Manitoba, was a small farming and ranching town of two thousand people 45 miles [72 km] north of the border in the valley of the Red River. It happens to have been my hometown. The thick black loam made for some of the finest agricultural soil in the world. Ten miles [16 km] to the west of Morris was a squalid American enclave that your expatriates nicknamed Freedom Town. At this time, we Manitobans were better off than most because of the flourishing wheat crops that underpinned our economy. But the Americans in Freedom Town were malnourished, and some were on the verge of starvation. To make matters worse, more Americans kept arriving at the camp.

The leader of Freedom Town was a firebrand who kept stirring his people up, pointing out that it was not right for Americans to face malnutrition, if not starvation, while a few miles down the road Canadians were enjoying the bounty that global warming had denied to Americans.

On April 30, 2046, a band of well-armed and well-lubricated Americans from Freedom Town entered Morris and seized its police station, municipal offices, and power and water plants. The Americans arrested and jailed the civil authorities in the small town. They raided Morris's supermarket and liquor store and helped themselves. Once the Americans had control of Morris, Freedom Town emptied out and its residents quickly established themselves there.

Our government had been expecting an incident that would bring conflict between Canadians and illegal American immigrants out into the open. We sent a corps of Royal Canadian Mounted Police into Morris and a battle ensued with significant losses on both sides. Our Mounties had not realized how well armed the Americans were, nor how well they would fight. Many of them were veterans of the various Middle East wars in which America had engaged early in the century. They were now in their fifties and sixties but had not forgotten how to fight.

In the end, however, the Freedom Town fighters were no match for our Mounties. As they closed in on the Americans, the Battle of Morris began to turn into the kind of last stand you Americans had made at the Alamo. Except that this time the embattled and surrounded Americans were able to call in reinforcements from U.S. troops stationed on your side of the border, waiting for just such an incident to give them the excuse to cross over in force.

America sent an armored brigade rolling across the border and up Highway 75 toward Morris. It took your armor only two hours to travel the 45 miles [72 km] and begin to rout our Mounties, who had not been prepared to engage tanks. When the smoke cleared, thirty-five Americans from Freedom Town and five soldiers had lost their lives, but two hundred Mounties and six Canadian civilians had died.

Word of the American incursion spread quickly. Canadians demanded that their government retaliate, and on May 5, 2046, Canada declared war on the United States. Of course, our government knew this was a futile effort, as you vastly outnumbered us and had a much stronger military. Still, honor demanded that we fight. And, our officials believed, if we fought, we would be able to negotiate better terms than if we surrendered without a struggle. It seems that it never entered the minds of our leaders that they would preside over the loss of Canadian sovereignty.

Canadian fighter-bombers from 17 Wing Winnipeg left their base at the airfield, most headed for the camps that the U.S. Army had established near Morris. But some Canadian planes crossed the border and bombed the North Dakota bases from which the armored column had come. No sooner had the first bombs fallen on American soil than the United States declared war on Canada. A squadron of your ultra-supersonic Aurora fighters took off from their base in Minot, North Dakota, quickly destroying the outmatched Canadian planes that it could find in the air, then flew on to destroy our remaining aircraft on the ground in Winnipeg. In half a day, America had command of the skies over central Canada. But that was just the beginning.

We later learned that America had prepared several different war plans for the conquest of Canada, one of which began with just the sort of cross-border rescue mission that occurred at Morris. There is no doubt that, if such an incident had not occurred on its own, sooner or later the U.S. would have provoked one.

A major goal of War Plan Maple was for victory over Canada to be as bloodless as possible. The U.S. did not intend to defeat the Canadian Army and then withdraw from our territory, as the victors in the world wars of the last century had done. Your goal was rather to incorporate Canada into the United States—to make our provinces states in your Union and give more living room to your increasingly desperate people. The more Canadian blood spilled, the harder that would be, and the longer a state of enmity would last.

We Canadians could not believe how fast you Americans moved. Squadrons of the 101st Airborne Division parachuted onto the Winnipeg airfield and onto the huge rail hub there, within hours securing both with little opposition. We had the illusion that our long border and vast space would hamper your forces and give us time to organize a resistance. No doubt the Russians had thought the same thing before Hitler launched Barbarossa.

Canada was vast, true, but most of our transportation, military bases, factories, and population were located within 100 miles [160 km] or so of the border. For example, all east-west rail traffic in Canada had to pass through the big Winnipeg railyard. Once it fell into your hands, it was no longer possible for us to ship troops or matériel from one part of Canada to the other. You did not have to conquer and hold all of Canada, only a few strategic points.

Making that easier for you was that all our major seaports were located either along the Saint Lawrence River or inside the Strait of Juan de Fuca, the latter providing access to the big ports at Victoria and Vancouver. Once your warships had blockaded the entrances to the Saint Lawrence and the Strait of Juan de Fuca, Canada could no longer supply itself by sea. With transcontinental rail traffic shut down, without access to the sea, with our airports under U.S. control, not only was Canada sealed off from the outside, it was largely immobilized inside. Then you waited for our government to capitulate.

We Canadians had always been a peaceful people, never aggressive toward our neighbors—America was our only neighbor! We had served in the great World Wars and other conflicts when called and given a good account of ourselves, but, as the twenty-first century proceeded, with no enemies in sight, we had turned our swords into plowshares, to quote from the book of Isaiah. We did not have enough modern fighter planes, and those we had we bought from you, so you knew their strengths and weaknesses better than we did. Most of our aircraft were for transport, search and rescue, and the like. Once we might have been able to mount a credible fight against your forces, though we would have lost in the end, but by the 2040s we were a mouse to your elephant. Our only option was to try to get the best deal for Canada.

With all this in mind, a delegation from Ottawa, headed by Prime Minister Campbell, flew to Washington, D.C., to discuss peace terms. We asked that American forces withdraw from Canada and in return offered to grant joint citizenship to any Americans who applied, whether they had particular skills or not. American corporations would be chartered in Canada just as they are in your country. These were extraordinary concessions, a mark of the disparity in the might of our two countries. We never imagined that the United States would not accept terms so much in its favor. But you had another plan in mind and turned us down even though we told you it would mean further armed conflict. You allowed our delegation to return to Ottawa. Then the final stage of the war began.

Our three most important eastern cities are Montréal, Toronto, and our capital, Ottawa, each less than two hour's drive from the U.S. border. War Plan Maple laid out the rapid American takeover of each, and you followed that plan exactly. Auroras from your Niagara Falls Air Reserve Station took less than thirty minutes to reach and destroy our 8 Wing at Trenton, between Toronto and Montréal. We had not a single airworthy fighter left at Trenton. American paratroopers closed

Highway 401 between those two cities and Highway 417 between Montréal and Ottawa so that we could not transfer troops or supplies between those cities.

Armored tank columns rolled around the western end of Lake Ontario and entered Toronto, meeting only light resistance from our weakened forces. Elements of your 1st Armored Division roared into Montréal, quickly securing it as well. Another U.S. force advanced up Highway 416 and into Ottawa, where it met stiff resistance, our government having decided we were honor-bound not to surrender our capital without a fight.

The Battle of Ottawa lasted eleven days. Even though we knew we could not possibly win against American might, our soldiers elected to go down fighting. Not only did they battle to the end, civilians rose up in the kind of insurgent guerrilla warfare you had experienced early in the century in Iran, Iraq, Afghanistan, Libya, and Venezuela. Losses on both sides were heavy, but since you could bring in unlimited reinforcements and we could not, the outcome was a foregone conclusion.

Once you put down the insurrection, you presented your terms. You would maintain military bases at various points in Canada of your choosing for the indefinite future. As soon as both sides signed the peace treaty, a number of American troops would withdraw to those bases, but most would be sent home. The sea blockade and the rail closure would end at the same time. The U.S. would grant American citizenship to all Canadians, and we would do the same for your citizens. All immigration restrictions would be dropped since everyone would have dual citizenship. The border would be open in both directions, just like the borders between two of our provinces or two of your states. Canadians could move to the U.S.; Americans could move to Canada. Then came the kicker.

Within twelve months, each Canadian province would conduct

a plebiscite to determine whether it wished to become an American state. In the first plebiscite, all Canadian provinces other than the Maritimes—New Brunswick, Nova Scotia, and Prince Edward Island—elected to join the United States. A year later, the Maritime provinces held a second plebiscite; this time they voted overwhelmingly to join the U.S. Thus by 2050, Canada had ceased to exist as a nation, each of its provinces now one of the United States of America.

Naturally, hard feelings among Canadians lasted for years; even today, some old-timers are bitter. It is hard to forget the images of our CC-277 Globemasters, which had flown so many peaceful missions around the world, the red maple leaf emblazoned on their fuselages, going up in flames at CFB Trenton. But people born after midcentury have never known anything but American citizenship and are proud of it.

Governor Fraser, before we close, in my research I have learned that back in the tens and twenties, pundits would try to pick which countries would be the so-called winners under global warming and which the so-called losers. How would you assess that thought for Canada? Is Canada a winner or a loser?

Well, as they say, it's complicated. We lost our sovereignty but won a good life as part of the United States. I'm sure some Canadians my age would say that was an enormous loss, while youngsters would say it was a win for Canada. But the temperature is still rising and some farmers along the former border are finding they can no longer make a living growing red winter wheat—the zone favorable for that has moved hundreds of miles north, and now we know it is going to keep on moving northward. So now it is the grandchildren of the former Canadians—the new Americans—who before long will no longer be growing wheat.

But the whole concept of winners and losers makes no sense anymore. You have told me about some of your other interviews and the destruction that global warming is causing around the world. Canada and some of the Scandinavian countries might still be able to claim they are winners, but how foolish and short-sighted that would be, when about the only thing we can be certain of is that next year, or the one after that, will be hotter than this year and so on into the future. The lesson from Canada, or from tiny Iceland, now a Chinese province, is that any country that appears to be winning just becomes a target for takeover by a larger and more powerful loser, until every country loses. There will be no winners.

Father Haile Moges is priest of the Church of Narga Selassie on Dek Island in Lake Tana, source of the Blue Nile in Ethiopia. In recognition of the site's peaceful setting, the name of the church translates as "Trinity of the Rest." I reached Father Moges via a generator-powered satellite videophone taken to the island by colleagues from Addis Ababa. Father Moges is the person to tell us about the critical events in Ethiopia, for he is an expert on the country's past.

Father, in spite of Ethiopia's long and proud history, the rest of the world has largely forgotten your country.

I thank you for finding me on an island in the middle of a nearly unknown lake in a country that the world has indeed forgotten. I have no contact with the outside world anymore, and therefore I am glad to speak with you.

Ethiopia is one of the oldest countries in the world. We trace our history back to the reign of Emperor Menelik I around 1000 BC. Herodotus said that "Egypt is a gift of the Nile." However, we Ethiopians feel that since almost all the water in the Nile rises in our land, it would be better to say, "Egypt is a gift of Ethiopia." Without our Nile, only nomads could inhabit the burning sands of Egypt.

The Blue Nile rises here at Lake Tana and flows across Ethiopia to meet the White Nile at Khartoum in Sudan. The Nile is more than 4,100 miles [6,600 km] long, the longest river in the world. It runs through eleven different African countries. Yet the country at the very end wound up with all the water. Usually it is those upstream who gain the right to water and decide how much to let flow downstream. How did it come to be reversed in Ethiopia? Ask the British.

In 1902, Britain had forced Ethiopia, then an independent kingdom, to accept a water treaty that said—I have the text here somewhere—ah: "His Majesty the Emperor Menelik II, King of Kings of Ethiopia, engages himself towards the Government of His Britannic Majesty not to construct, or allow to be constructed, any work across the Blue Nile, Lake Tana, or the Sobat, which would arrest the flow of their waters into the Nile except in agreement with His Britannic Majesty's Government and the Government of the Sudan." Such was the language of imperial power.

Then, in the aftermath of World War I, in 1922 Britain granted Egypt independence. When the Nile countries met in 1929 to divide the river waters, Britain played favorites and directed its colonies—Sudan, Uganda, Kenya, and Tanzania—to cede all their water rights to Egypt. That agreement lasted until 1959, when the Nile countries amended it to give Sudan about 24 percent of the water, but no more to Ethiopia. The pact reiterated the one of 1902, saying that the upriver countries could not build dams, irrigation works, or hydroelectric plants without Egypt's approval. Egypt had veto power over our fate and our future. How is that fair?

By 1959, the United States and the Soviet Union were using poor African countries as pawns in their Cold War. During the Suez Crisis, the USSR agreed to help Egypt build Nasser's huge dam at Aswan. The United States retaliated by sending experts from your Bureau of Reclamation to help Ethiopia locate sites for our own hydroelectric dams. They identified several good locations on the Blue Nile inside our country. If we built those dams, we could shut off the flow of the Nile to Sudan and Egypt just by closing valves. That threat led Egyptian president Anwar Sadat to issue a warning in 1979: "We are not go-

ing to wait to die of thirst in Egypt. We'll go to Ethiopia and die there."
Sadat was seeking a détente with Israel and had promised to divert
the Nile into the Sinai Desert to benefit the Jewish state. In response,
Ethiopia, led by the evil tyrant Mengistu—that one is surely burning
in hell—threatened to block the Blue Nile. It was a dangerous time.

Of course, Africa's ultimate problem has always been its large population. Even without global warming, the presence of so many people
might have sealed our doom eventually. In 2000, the population of the
four lower-Nile countries of Egypt, Sudan, Ethiopia, and Uganda had
grown to 188 million people. The Nile was already in trouble because
of the population increase but also because of pollution and the early
effects of global warming. Egypt's population alone was increasing by
a million people every six months. By 2040, the number of people in
the four countries had more than doubled. But for all those extra people there was no more food and, because of global warming, even less
water. Each person had to get by on less food and water than their
predecessors, and even that had not been enough.

We had built dams on some of the sites your engineers had rec-
ommended back in the 1960s. The Nile Basin Initiative countries, with
Egypt abstaining, had agreed that Ethiopia could build those dams.
Far downstream from Lake Tana, just 9 miles [15 km] above the Sudanese border, where the Nile is a much larger river, lay another site that
would loom large in this century: It was to have been named the Mil-
lennium Dam, but we renamed it the Grand Ethiopian Renaissance
Dam. That name tells you what the dam meant to Ethiopia. It was to
power a million homes and still have power left over to sell to other
African nations. As you say, it would put Ethiopia on the map at last.

We surveyed the site and had the dam design ready in 2010, but
we kept our plans secret until a month before we laid the foundation
stone. You can imagine the reaction of the Egyptians. You see, when

you build a new dam you do not create any more water; only God can do that. To fill the new reservoir, you have to hold back water that would have previously flowed downstream. That meant that Egypt would receive even less of the already depleted flow of the river, her life's blood. This led Egypt's leader to remind the United Nations in 2019 that "The Nile is a question of life, a matter of existence to Egypt." Those are words that nations use when they want to get their country-men ready for war.

As always with big projects, the dam cost more money and took longer than projected, but finally we opened it and had a big celebra-tion. We had promised to fill the reservoir as slowly as feasible, cutting the flow to Egypt no more than necessary, after which we would make sure that she got her agreed-to share. And for a while she did. But by the 2040s, global warming had slowed the flow of the Nile enough so that if we gave Egypt her full share, the level of the reservoir and the amount of water going through our power turbines would drop and reduce our electricity production and sales. We could even foresee a time when the reservoir might stop generating any electricity at all. So we began to hold some water back, then more and more, in violation of the agreement. Egypt issued an ultimatum: Unless the gates on all the dams on the Blue and White Nile above Sudan were opened as specified in the agreement, she would consider it an act of war and take appropriate action. Each of the Nile countries began to mobilize troops and conduct military exercises.

Unbeknownst to the nine upstream countries, the two farthest downstream, Egypt and Sudan, had secretly agreed to come to each other's aid in the event of a war over the Nile. The two countries moved troops to the Sudanese border, where they faced Ethiopian soldiers across a no-man's-land. Uganda placed its troops under Ethiopian command to help resist an imminent invasion from Egypt and Sudan.

On the night of May 15, 2040, Egyptian commandos crossed the

Sudanese-Ethiopian border and blew up the Grand Ethiopian Renaissance Dam, releasing a huge surge of water downstream, most of which flowed wasted into the Mediterranean. Ethiopia and the other Nile countries promptly declared war on both Egypt and Sudan. We Ethiopians were confident we could win because for a century we had been fighting almost continuously with each other, with Italians, Somalians, Eritreans, and with whomever we could find to fight. We had essentially become a warrior state. We believed that the Egyptians and Sudanese were soft and no match for us. That belief did not last long.

Countries like Iran, North Korea, and Pakistan, even though they had professed their commitment to abolishing nuclear weapons, in fact had been building them as fast as they could and selling them on the black market to any country or group who could afford them. The North Koreans would design a weapon to the customer's specifications: uranium or plutonium; tactical or strategic; this many or that many kilotons; air-blast or impact-triggered—whatever the customer desired. Egypt had purchased several atomic bombs from the North Koreans and as the situation grew more tense, Egypt announced that it had enough atomic weapons loaded on fueled bombers to destroy every capital in East Africa. Egypt demanded that Ethiopia and Uganda surrender, or else she would destroy those capitals one by one starting with Addis Ababa and Kampala.

If you remember your history, you will recall that near the end of the twentieth-century war with Japan, many believed that the United States, instead of bombing Japan, should have dropped a demonstration atomic bomb to reveal the awful power of its new weapon. But you did not, and instead destroyed Hiroshima and Nagasaki.

When our leaders scoffed at the threat, the Egyptians conducted their own demonstration by dropping a 1 kiloton tactical bomb on the Eritrean island of Dahlak Kebir in the Red Sea, which had once belonged to us. The air burst obliterated the island and its three thousand inhabitants, which included many Ethiopians, but produced little fallout. We blustered for two days, but we had no atomic weapons and our intelligence told us that the Egyptians were preparing to use more of theirs. We and Uganda surrendered to the Egyptians and Sudanese, whose troops quickly occupied both countries and whose engineers took control of our dams and power plants.

In better times, the threat of even the most limited nuclear war would have brought international condemnation and mobilized an all-out effort among nations to find a peaceful solution. But by this time, the United Nations and its International Atomic Energy Agency had ceased to exist. There was no longer any international peacekeeping force. The United States could not afford to act as the world's policeman. No nation on its own had both the means and the will to come to the aid of a poor country in the Horn of Africa. In any case, a war that involved a few tactical nuclear weapons in our remote region would not produce dangerous global fallout. So, the rest of the world looked the other way and left East Africa to clean up its own mess. The Nile War revealed the true cost of the twenty-first-century breakdown in world order. Rogue nations learned that there was no one to stop them from doing as they pleased.

We had feared that the Egyptians would colonize Ethiopia, but they withdrew most of their troops, leaving only garrisons at the sites of the dams and power plants to make sure we could not again close the gates. Given the widespread famine that by then had swept Ethiopia, what sane country would have wanted to adopt our problems?

Already at the turn of the century, although we grew wheat, maize, barley, sorghum, and millet for our own use and for export, half of Ethiopians were undernourished. Those faces on your TV screens were our faces. Our coffee was world famous, but as international trade collapsed, there was no way to get it to markets abroad, and people can survive without coffee—it is a luxury and the time for luxury had passed. The higher temperatures and shrinking water supplies not only here but across sub-Saharan Africa have led to widespread starvation.

Those who stood by and allowed the Earth to heat doomed Ethiopia. They should have heeded our great 1930s leader, for whom my parents named me, Haile Selassie: "Throughout history, it has been the inaction of those who could have acted; the indifference of those who should have known better; the silence of the voice of justice when it mattered most; that has made it possible for evil to triumph."

PART 6
FASCISM AND
MIGRATION

Professor Sinclair Thomas is a scholar of twenty-first-century fascism. I spoke with him at his home in Toronto in the American state of Ontario.

Professor Thomas, at the turn of the century it would have seemed ludicrous to talk about such a thing as twenty-first-century fascism. It seemed to have almost disappeared, like Marxism, among outmoded and failed political systems.

Yes, the resurrection of fascism is just one of a thousand things that have happened that no one foresaw when the century began. But with twenty-twenty hindsight, we can see that there were inklings of the potential return of fascism in the increase in anti-immigration sentiment that was getting started back in those days. Eventually, the prospect of being overrun by hordes of starving, thirsty, sick climate refugees with nothing to lose led many richer countries to turn to a strongman and ultimately to fascism to protect themselves and their borders. Of course, it did not work, but once a fascist leader gains power, they prove hard to get rid of short of revolution or war.

One can trace the roots of neo-fascism to the first decade, when both legal and illegal immigration were rising around the world. The U.S. had its Mexicans; the Germans their Turks and Croats; the Brits their Pakistanis and Indians, and so forth. During the 2020s, strong anti-immigration movements had appeared in most developed countries. As heat and drought caused crop failures and widespread famine, the number of desperate climate refugees rose dramatically.

Rich countries resisted and their anti-immigration movements grew stronger.

The threat was greatest wherever a relatively rich country shared a border with a relatively poor one: the United States and Mexico; India and Bangladesh; Libya and Niger; Egypt and Sudan; South Africa and Mozambique; South and North Korea; Brazil and Bolivia. And, Spain and Morocco, separated only by a short stretch of the Mediterranean Sea. In the better-off country in each pair, nationalistic, anti-immigrant attitudes became too strong for traditional political parties to ignore. Their platforms became more fascist and, in some countries, as in America, new parties rose to threaten the traditional ones.

We former Canadians were an exception, as our only land border was with the U.S. We had always been friendly to immigrants partly because they could only get here by plane, which allowed us to control the numbers. We took note of your failed efforts to control your southern border with Mexico. Little did we imagine that in a few decades Americans trying to sneak into Canada would be the illegal immigrants.

At the turn of the century, the notion that fascism might appear again would have seemed like a sick joke to most scholars and politicians. To label a person or a government fascist was the worst of insults. Yet by the 2040s, a League of Fascist Nations proudly bore the emblem of the fasces, the bundle of rods that was the ancient Roman symbol of authority and the icon of the Italian fascists of the 1920s and 1930s under Mussolini.

The global rise of fascism is too large a subject for one conversation—I and others have written entire books about it—so I will focus on what happened here in North America. That will demonstrate how fascism can arise even in a democracy. It should have been no surprise; after all, Germany in the early 1930s was a democracy.

At first, the movement that was to become appealed to national unity, pride, job access, and cultural identity, each of which bolstered the anti-immigration sentiment that had become a hot-button political issue by the first two decades of this century. Right-wing politicians, pundits, and demagogues of every stripe began to demonize Mexican immigrants even as the economies of states like California and Texas had come to depend on their labor. Arizona and other states passed laws that allowed police to demand that those they suspected of being in the country illegally—just suspected, no probable cause necessary—show their papers, a practice that smacked of Gestapo tactics. These anti-Mexican sentiments led to the erection of your border wall and other expensive but futile measures along the border.

These actions accomplished three things. First, they offended Mexico, producing hatred that would haunt the two countries as relations between them broke down. Second, they forced Mexicans to invent other ways of getting into the United States, which they were very clever at doing. Third, the less effective the barriers became at keeping out immigrants, the angrier American demagogues became, the louder their voices rose, as did the number of people who supported them. Fascism requires an enemy, preferably one who can appear to be dangerous but in fact is close to helpless compared to the might of the state. Mexicans fit the bill.

At first, the foes of immigration found a home in the Republican Party, where they helped elect Donald Trump three times. But as the movement became more vocal and extreme, in the late 2020s the anti-immigration forces split off to form the America First Party, taking its name from the isolationist movement led by aviator Charles Lindbergh in the years just before the Japanese attack on Pearl Harbor. By the 2028 election, people had begun to abandon the Republican Party, blaming the party for its decades-long denial of the scientific truth of global warming and its failure to prepare the country for it. During the thirties, the Republican Party effectively disappeared from American politics.

In that election, America First made a far stronger showing than any third party in American history. America First's appeal to nationalism and its anti-immigrant rhetoric had grown so strident that no thinking person could any longer doubt that the party stood for drastic, though unspecified, measures against immigrants. The record third-party vote caused the two majority parties, including the Democrats, to become even more anti-immigrant, all the while draping themselves in the flag and waving the Bible.

Polls showed that the America First candidate Jared Buchanan would win the next election by a substantial margin. Soon both Republicans and Democrats had begun to swap their lapel-pin flags for America First buttons. Republicans tried to deny they had ever denied global warming, saying they had only asked for more scientific evidence, but it fooled no one.

In 2032, Buchanan won in a landslide and America First earned a veto-proof majority in both houses of Congress. Within weeks, his photograph began to appear not just in government buildings, as the president's image always had, but in many offices, homes, and schools. Those buttons were seen everywhere—even schoolchildren began to wear them. The America First salute—a clenched right fist held over the heart—began to replace the handshake.

One of the first pieces of legislation the new Congress passed was the America First Act, which called for the deportation of all illegal immigrants. Each American citizen was required to have in his or her possession an identity card and to display it on demand.

Business owners who employed immigrants without papers risked going to prison and a large fine. These noncitizens were deemed not to have the right of habeas corpus and were to be deported immediately without benefit of trial. If a person had no ID card and an on-the-spot, fifteen-minute DNA test showed them to be of Mexican descent, they were on their way back to Mexico within days, and a pleasant journey it was not. The government nationalized railroad companies and used them to collect and ship Mexicans without identity papers in railcars back to Mexico. Many did not survive the trip. Those who did languished in border refugee camps, and large numbers died there, as Mexico had no way to care for them. Horrible pictures emerged showing emaciated Mexicans begging for food and parents who were separated from their children at camp gates, as happened a century earlier at the gates of Auschwitz.

The America First Act was designed to rid the United States of illegal immigrants, but that did not slake the anger of the most rabid America Firsters. California, the Southwest, and Texas were feeling the effects of global warming, as water supplies shrank and the ever-rising heat killed crops in the fields. With the illegals mostly gone, party leaders needed to find someone new to blame. Who else but citizens of Mexican descent? This led to the Americans Only Act, modeled on the Nuremberg Laws of the 1930s. The act classified citizens along racial lines and was sufficiently complicated that the government had to issue charts in English and Spanish to explain it, using brown, white, and tan circles. People were classified American if all four of their grandparents were of "American blood" (white circles). They were "Mexican" if three or four of their grandparents were Mexican (brown circles). A person with one or two Mexican grandparents had mixed blood (tan circles).

Strangely, to the America Firsters, ridding the country of all illegal immigrants only made things worse. Now not only were they unavail-

able to take the blame for the country's ills, there was no one to per-
form menial, low-wage tasks. Strawberries and lettuce rotted in the
fields of California, Arizona, and Texas; restaurants in the Southwest
had to close; schools emptied; dirt and trash piled up in office buildings. What had been an impending economic collapse soon became
a reality.

The leaders of the America First Party had assumed that, as the
government confiscated Mexican property and drove out Mexican
business owners, jobs previously held by them would open up, allowing deserving Americans to step in and take over those jobs. But
by this time, in the late 2030s, the American economy—and, for that
matter, the world economy—was so depressed that typically no one
saw any benefit to adopting one of the abandoned businesses and trying to run it at a profit. Moreover, even in those hard times too few
Americans were willing to take up the menial tasks that immigrants
had once performed.

Without obvious enemies and with the American economy in tat-
ters, in the 2040s people turned away from the America First brand of
fascism. Not necessarily to some other party, but more often because
they lost interest and saw no point in voting. In the last election in
which America First ran a candidate, 2044, only 19 percent of eligible
voters cast a ballot. Today, of course, the percentage is even lower.
Unfortunately, in countries that were not true democracies, fascism
lasted much longer, though eventually, as people had to focus more
on their own survival, they had less time to spend blaming minorities
and immigrants, and fascism lost its appeal in those countries as well.

Today, in most areas of the world, politics has become irrelevant.
Why bother to vote when you know that leaders of the past failed humanity and brought doomsday within sight?

Raul Fuentes was Mexico's last ambassador to the United States before relations between the two countries collapsed.

Ambassador Fuentes, take us through the years when relations between Mexico and the U.S. broke down.

You will pardon me, please, if my English has deteriorated in the decades since I spoke it every day while stationed in your country. For us diplomats, English was a second language. We often spoke it among ourselves, just to show off our command. Nowadays, no self-respecting Mexican would be caught dead speaking English. So, forgive me if I have forgotten too much of mine.

Proximidad can make for great friendships, but for nations it can also make great enemies. One of your poets wrote of good fences making good neighbors. That was long before you built your despicable border fence and wall, of course. The relations of our two countries have swung back and forth between friendship and animosity over our entire history. But miraculously, we came to war only once, in 1846. Sadly, we were no match for *el Norte* then or later.

We do like to remind you that while your West was still terra incognita, our Aztec ancestors had built a flourishing civilization. It was our fate and misfortune to lie downstream on your main western river, *el Río Colorado*—named by a Spaniard long before you arrived. One of our leaders said it well: "Poor Mexico, so far from God, and so close to the United States!" Had *el Rió Colorado* flowed north out of Mexico and into the United States, leaving us upstream from you, quite a few things in history would have been different and more to our advantage.

For millions of years, the river had flowed south and west and delivered its water to the Gulf of California, where it built a great delta. Until we began irrigating near Mexicali and Calexico, we did not need water from the river. As soon as we did, you exercised the right of the man upstream and kept the water for yourselves. After you built the Hoover Dam, you generously decreed that instead of the 100 percent of *el Rió Colorado* water that God had given Mexico, you would allow her 10 percent. What could we do? *Algo es algo; menos es nada*—half a loaf is better than none, you say. Your laws said that in drought times your states would share the burden of providing us the water you had promised. But we knew that until the agreement was tested, it was just words on paper. History tells us that when drought comes, people keep the water they control, no matter what treaties say. Given your prejudices against Mexico, your demonizing of our poor, we saw no reason to believe you would behave differently.

By the beginning of this century, you were using every drop of your share of *el Rió Colorado*. Still you allowed *loco* growth and development in your western cities and towns. We have a saying, *"Procura lo mejor, espera lo peor y toma lo que viniere"*—hope for the best but prepare for the worst. You in *el Norte* could manage only the first half of that proverb. You thought that because you had stored two or three years of the river's annual flow in your reservoirs, you could survive any drought. You did not believe, or could not afford to believe, that drought would one day drain your reservoirs.

You continued to provide Mexico with its 10 percent until the 2030s. By then, global warming and growing population had caused your reservoirs to run low, but we insisted you keep sending us our share. We were not the only ones to demand a share of the river. Your

Native Americans, particularly the huge Navajo tribe, also began to insist on a larger share and sued your government to get it. You faced a hard choice. You could continue to send water down the river and onto our fields south of the border, but then you would have to deny that water to your Imperial Valley alfalfa growers and soon to your cities. In other words, you would have to take water flowing under the noses of Americans and give it to Mexicans and Native Americans. As you say, "fat chance." Instead you announced that the United States would "temporarily" curtail water deliveries below the border and restore them when more water was available. Even then your politicians denied the reality of *el calentamiento global*.

We knew, of course, when "temporary" would end—sometime in the twenty-second century, if not the twenty-third, and we really preferred not to have to wait that long. Without the water from the Colorado, Mexican agriculture at the border, already in danger from the rising heat, would die, many of our farmers would go out of business, and our people would go hungry. The way things were looking for the rest of the century, without that produce not only would we not have the revenue from the crops but famine was a real possibility as well.

Whenever America wanted to keep people from crossing the border to the north, or water from crossing to the south, you built a wall or dam and dared them to do something about it. You had an utter disregard for us Mexicans as people—people just like you who, as fate and fortune would have it, wound up on one side of a line in the sand rather than the other. In intent the United States may not have been racist, but in practice you were, and intentions do not matter.

But we were not without our methods of response. *Quien teme la muerte no goza la vida*—cowards die many times—we say, and Mexicans are not cowards. The water treaty between us not only covered *el Río Colorado*, it required Mexico to deliver to the United States several hundred thousand acre-feet each year from Mexican tributaries to the *Río Bravo del Norte*—the Rio Grande, you call it. When you cut off the flow of the Colorado, we did the same to the *Río Bravo*.

We tried diplomacy but got nowhere, so we took the only action open: In 2032 we sued the United States in the International Court of Justice in The Hague, on the grounds that you had violated both the water-quantity and water-quality provisions of our treaty. Stationed in Washington, I was deeply involved in that confrontation. By then the United Nations was declining in importance each year and, although the court found for Mexico, there was no means to enforce the ruling. Your government announced that you no longer recognized the World Court. The UN Security Council voted on a motion to force the United States to return the flow of the Colorado River and pay reparations to Mexico, but you used your veto to stop the motion. America continued to block the flow of the Colorado until our Mexicali and Calexico agricultural districts returned to barren deserts. Today hardly anyone remembers the onions, *verde y suculento*, the asparagus, beets, and lettuce that we grew in the Mexicali fields, much of which we shipped north to you.

Beyond holding back water in the *Río Bravo*, we had no choice but to use the few other weapons we had. Your cities of Phoenix and Las Vegas, both located far from salt water, had paid to build desalting plants on the Gulf of California, in our country. You would give us the desalted water the plants produced, and we would give you the same amount from our treaty share of the river water. By 2045, two of the plants were operating and two more were under construction. Their cost was around $1.5 billion each, but since *el agua es vida*, to a man with a great thirst, water is cheap at any price. After your government shut off the flow of the Colorado River to Mexico, we had no share of the river left to give—you had already taken it. Since you had broken your side of the bargain, we felt no need to keep ours, so we nationalized the desalting plants, retaining all the water they produced for ourselves. It turned out we could operate the plants as well as you—we already were! America responded by freezing Mexican assets in the United States; we nationalized all U.S. factories in Mexico and withdrew from the U.S.-Mexico-Canada Trade Agreement.

One major plank of your fascist platform was that the United States should deport not only all illegal Mexicans but all legal ones who could not pass your racial-identity test. You began to round up Mexicans and transport them to camps near the border, where they were processed before being shipped across. What your inept Department of Homeland Purity and your fascist *demagogos* had not understood was just how big a job that would be and what side effects it would have. No one even knew how many illegals were in your country at the time, but in California alone there were an estimated 5 million. After you rounded up the first few hundred thousand, word began to spread that the border camps were full of dysentery, cholera, and typhus. When the remaining millions of Mexicans in California and Texas heard of the mass deaths in the camps, many decided that the only way to save themselves and their families was to make it back to Mexico on their own and avoid the camps. The Mexicans developed a network to get people out of the States. Its code word was *Salsipuedes*—get out if you can. Within six months after the roundups began, an estimated 2 million Mexicans and their families with whatever belongings they could carry or cart were on the roads of California. In Texas, another million were on the move. And so were others from nearly every state in the Union. California's roads and freeways quickly clogged, and nothing went anywhere except on foot. At the height of the crisis, your National Guard and troops from the Mexican Army faced each other across the border, and war appeared imminent. But it was too late to save many of the deportees. In the camps on your side of the border, many hundreds of thousands of Mexicans died; on our side, the same, for we had even less ability to care for the desperate refugees than you did.

Now señor, you must forgive me, for I have become too emotional to continue. Remembering is too hard on an old man. I must bid you adios.

PART 7
HEALTH

Dr. Charles Block was the director of Médecins Sans Frontières. I interviewed him at his home in Geneva.

Dr. Block, how has global warming affected human health over this century?

Some people call it the century of heat, others the century of fire, the century of flood, and so on. I call it the century of death. I am a physician and spent my entire career working for MSF on the front lines in countries all over the world, retiring in 2070. I saw firsthand how global warming made nearly every aspect of human health worse and cost hundreds of millions of lives.

Even in the early years of this century, we knew global warming was going to cause a health crisis. In the tens and twenties there were dozens of reports testifying to that. But even we medical professionals underestimated the depth of that crisis.

It was obvious that global warming would cause more people to die from extreme heat, yet some thought that fewer would die from cold. But the two did not balance out, and far more died from heat than were saved from the cold. At the turn of the century, some areas were already so hot that if they got hotter, hundreds of thousands were bound to perish. In the pre-monsoon summer months during the twentieth century, the highs in the plains of the Indus and Ganges Rivers in India, Pakistan, and Bangladesh often reached 113°F [45°C]. Today those highs routinely reach 124°F [51°C] and are often even a few degrees higher. Most of the area remained rural where people have no access to air-conditioning or even to the electricity needed to power a fan. In such regions, heat mortality shot up. Things were even worse in the cities, where metal, asphalt, and concrete soak up heat during the day and release it at night. Before global warming really got going, a typical large city would be several degrees warmer than the surrounding rural area. As the world got hotter, the cities got hotter still, especially at night, and many in the developing countries became death traps.

In 2000, the World Health Organization projected that a 1.8°F [1°C] temperature rise would kill an additional 300,000 people annually, but by now global temperatures have risen four times that. A rough estimate is that in the second half of this century 5 to 6 million people above the late twentieth-century average have died annually from the direct effects of heat. But the toll is rising. By 2100, it will likely be roughly several million higher and go on increasing after that.

Malnutrition has been another major killer. At the beginning of this century, at least 3 million children died of malnutrition annually, but vastly more were vulnerable to even a slight drop in food production. Global warming has made malnutrition worse in several ways, some of which had not been anticipated. As the century went on, extreme weather events grew more common—both heat and precipitation—drowning some agricultural areas and drying up others. When transportation systems began to break down midcentury, it became harder and harder to move crops from the fields to the marketplace. In many areas, pests proliferated as the temperature rose. The heat reduced food production because people could not work the fields during most of the daylight hours. I estimate that today between 15 and 20 million people die annually from poor nutrition.

Let me now turn to disease. The Intergovernmental Panel on Climate Change, the World Health Organization, and others had tried to project the effect of global warming on illness, but it was hard to do because there were so many unknowns. Take the example of malaria. Back in the 2010s, each year more than 200 million people got malaria and nearly 500,000 died from it, 90 percent of them in Africa. The population at risk of malaria even without global warming was projected back then to double by 2100, and with global warming, the death toll has risen even more. The mosquitoes that transmit the disease have a small temperature range in which they can best breed. A little cooler, and their growth is stunted or they die. A little warmer, and they flourish, but when the temperature rises out of their range, they cannot breed, and die out. You might have thought these would offset each other, but the additional factor was that as temperature rose, areas that had previously been too cold for mosquitoes were no longer so. And in those areas, the population had not developed resistance to the disease and so were more vulnerable. Thus, global warming has caused many more deaths from malaria than had been forecast.

Ticks are another lethal insect that are highly temperature dependent. The tick life cycle is complicated, but with hindsight we can see what has happened. First, let's remember just how pestilent the tick is. There are a number of species that collectively carry Lyme disease, tularemia, Rocky Mountain spotted fever, Colorado tick fever, and more. As temperatures rose, as with malaria, disease-carrying ticks spread into areas that had previously been too cold for them. Ticks have now infested former Canadian provinces that had not known them before and are moving ever northward. They have disappeared in more southerly areas but there has been a net increase in the number of ticks and infections.

War is obviously a health issue directly and indirectly. It has cost hundreds of millions of lives and in the case of the Indo–Pakistani War, rendered vast areas uninhabitable. One threat related to war that

Médecins Sans Frontières did not fully anticipate was the worsening health of the millions of climate refugees, who often wound up without sanitation, food, water, or medical services. Our studies did not envision that fascist governments would impound millions of deportees in squalid and deadly border camps. Nor did they consider the effects of worldwide flooding on dysentery, cholera, yellow fever, and typhus. Nor that already dry regions such as the American Southwest, the Sahel between the Sahara and the Sudanian Savanna, and parts of China, for example, would become so dry that the land would begin to blow away on the wind, creating famine and, for those living downwind, lethal respiratory problems. Nor that radiation poisoning from the Indo–Pakistani War would spread death throughout the Punjab for decades. Nor the higher mortality among seniors, especially in fascist countries, some of which began to practice euthanasia of the elderly. So, you see why our estimates early in the century of the coming ill health and mortality were so low.

Organizations like MSF and the Red Cross depended on the donations of caring people. Plenty still care, but few have the means to give to even the most-worthy charity. Most need whatever they have to support their own families. The combination of shrinking resources and a ballooning health crisis seems sure to close both MSF and the Red Cross before the century is out.

This may have seemed a bit like a dry recitation of numbers. If so, I have failed to convey the impact of the greatest health crisis in human history. Remember that we are talking about the lives of countless human beings, not numbers, but individual men, women, and especially children. Let me give you one example that occurred while I was stationed at an MSF hospital in Morelos, Mexico, during the 2040s, one I will never forget. A ten-year-old girl was brought in by people who had found her abandoned by the side of the road near noon on one of the hottest days of July. They did not know her name, but believed she was a deportee from the United States. The girl showed symptoms of severe malaria, and just as I started to examine her, she died in my hands. My job then was to fill out her death certificate and the cause of death. In addition to malaria, she was malnourished near the point of starvation, severely dehydrated, running a high fever, her body covered with infected sores from tick and mosquito bites, her legs covered with watery excrement from dysentery. So, which one should I have chosen as the cause of death? I remember turning away and scribbling something down and moving on to the next patient, thinking to myself that I knew the ultimate cause of her death: the criminal indifference of the people who could have done something to stop global warming and save her and countless others but did not bother to go to the trouble.

Today I am talking to Dr. Margaret Sandlin, former executive direc-
tor of Death with Dignity, an Oregon-based nonprofit founded in the
1990s.

Dr. Sandlin, tell me about the origin of Death with Dignity and
how it evolved during this century.

We got our start in Oregon because it was the first state and one of the
first governments in the world to pass legislation legalizing medical
aid in dying. We believed with Victor Hugo that "There is one thing
stronger than all the armies of the world, and that is an idea whose
time has come." Our idea was and is that when living has become unbearable, people should be able to obtain legal medical assistance in
ending their lives. Of course, the idea was not original with us, but we
were one of the first to advocate and defend it as public policy.

To say that assisted dying was controversial would be a colossal
understatement. Early in the century, Attorney General John Ashcroft
had gone so far as to use federal drug agents to prosecute doctors who
helped terminally ill patients to die. This turned out to be a good thing
for us because it got the matter before the Supreme Court, which
voted 6 to 3 that Ashcroft had exceeded his authority. We then took
our cause to other states, and by 2020 Oregon, California, Vermont,
and Washington allowed assisted dying.

Let me emphasize that, since the start, we advocated that only
those with a terminal, diagnosed medical illness should be able to
end their lives and only with a doctor's assistance. Of course, that

depended on the definition of "terminal" and of "illness," both of which were about to change.

Through the twenties and thirties, we had success in one state after another and our organization grew. By around 2040, our staff and medical professionals in the southern states began to meet patients who did not present with our typical profile. They came in on their own, often with a letter from a psychologist. Let me give some background, especially for your readers too young to have lived through this period.

Scholars had long known that the rate of suicide—here I am speaking of those who took their own lives without medical assistance—correlated directly with temperature. By the mid-2040s, in the southernmost parts of the country, summer heat waves were lasting longer and reaching higher temperatures. This put additional stress on the elderly and infirm, people in nursing homes and assisted living facilities. We began to notice this first in Phoenix, where there was not enough electricity to keep the air conditioners running continuously and water was becoming scarce. Heat mortality in Phoenix was rising, especially among the elderly, whose resistance to any sort of stress was lower. After a bad heat wave, Phoenix undertakers had more business than they could handle.

In 2045, a Phoenix physician called on our office there to plead the case of one of his patients, a ninety-five-year-old woman in frail health. She did not have a diagnosed terminal illness, but suffered terribly during the incessant heat waves, when it was impossible for a bedridden person to get comfortable. He presented in writing his medical opinion that this patient would die of heatstroke in the next heat wave or the one after. In other words, he was stating that it was his opinion that she did have a condition that would prove terminal, just one we had not countenanced before. With the approval of her family, he was prepared to hasten her death to avoid the pain and suffering she would have to go through, but wanted the moral support, and, if necessary, the legal and financial support of Death with Dignity. We made no promises, but he took the action anyway. He was arrested, convicted of malpractice, and lost his license. After probably the longest and most difficult debate in our organization's history, our board agreed to underwrite an appeal of his conviction. His was evidently an idea whose time had come, as Hugo had written, because our campaign to support his legal expenses raised about twice what we had expected.

The appeal wound its way through the lower courts and by 2050 was on the verge of reaching the Supreme Court. To our surprise, the American Medical Association filed a brief on our behalf. When we met with the AMA to strategize, we learned that physicians all over the country were facing the same issue as that doctor: what to do about elderly patients who were bound to die an agonizing death in one form or another as a result of global warming. Elderly people with no money, no family, and nowhere to go were becoming trapped in doomed seashore communities and stifling cities like Phoenix. They had begun to kill themselves in horrific ways that I will not go into, as well as just dying of neglect and starvation, alone and forgotten. Adult children wanted to help their elderly parents, but often lacked the space and resources to take care of them. They came to us to find a decent way out for their fathers and mothers.

Legal cases that depended on the truth of man-made global warming had already come before the court, leading them to make it a matter of settled law: too late, but better than never. The next question was what to do about the present and future victims of global warming. In a rare unanimous vote, the court overturned the conviction of the Phoenix doctor, and he was reinstated and began to practice again. State after state started to revise their statutes to redefine "terminal illness" as he had.

Our organization was in the strange position of not wanting to be too successful, yet after that decision we had so many requests from every state that we had to expand. The number of assisted deaths rose sharply, but so did the self-inflicted suicides. In 2020, suicide was the tenth leading cause of death in the country. Back then, about one person in ten thousand killed themselves annually, totaling about 800,000 globally per year. Among those ages fifteen to twenty-nine, suicide was the second leading cause of death. Over three-quarters occurred in low- and middle-income countries, and in those cases, many had chosen the truly horrible method of ingesting pesticide.

By 2060, self-inflicted suicide had become the third leading cause of death globally, with heatstroke coming in second. By that time, no matter what people had thought about global warming before, it was undeniably happening and, unless one could come up with a good reason why it should stop, was going to continue and get worse. People in educated countries had grasped the concept of the CO_2 pipeline and knew that there was a lot of future warming left in it. They knew there would be no escape for them and their descendants for who knows how many generations.

Depression had always been a medical problem. Now it had become endemic and a sick joke started going around, "To be sane is to be depressed." The more the reality and the effectively eternal nature of global warming sank in, the more people took their own lives. There has always been a certain copycat aspect to suicide, sad to say, and now a person did not have to look far to find someone to copy in their own family, or among their friends and neighbors.

Now another doctor came to us about the case of a middle-aged man, a patient otherwise in good health who had become so depressed—one could have said terminally depressed—that he could not function. This man had appealed to the doctor to assist him in ending his life humanely and with dignity. Like many, he did not want his children to have to deal with his remains. We supported the doctor from the outset, as did the AMA, APA, and other medical organizations, arguing that depression had now reached the stage of a pandemic, justifying assisted dying on medical and humane grounds. This time there was no objection from any official quarter and doctors began to put the idea into practice.

What is the state of Death with Dignity today and what is its future?

I retired ten years ago but left the organization in good hands. Soon it will celebrate its one hundredth birthday. Death with Dignity has expanded far beyond anything our founders could have imagined and become a global organization. By the standards we used to use to judge business success, you would have to say we succeeded. It's odd to wish you hadn't needed to. As you can imagine, the work we do, meeting with families facing one of the hardest decisions anyone ever has to make, is terribly wearing on the staff. Our frontline workers cannot do it for long, else they too become terminally depressed. We used to depend a lot on volunteers, but few people seem to have time for volunteering nowadays. So, to answer your question, as much as I hate to say it, I don't see how Death with Dignity can go on much longer. The problem it tries to ease has become too enormous and too debilitating.

PART 8
SPECIES

Dr. Sandrine Landry is head of the International Union for Conservation of Nature based in Gland, Switzerland, near Geneva. Dr. Landry's scientific specialties are coral reefs and the ecology of Australia. I began by asking her about that continent; then we turned to worldwide extinctions.

Dr. Landry, we have learned how global warming affected the land and people of Australia. What has been the impact of global warming on Australia's unique ecosystems?

Let me start with the Great Barrier Reef off Australia's northeast state of Queensland. During the twentieth century, it was the country's most famous tourist attraction and the largest reef in the world, more than 1,200 miles [2,000 km] long, with an area greater than the United Kingdom and Ireland put together. It was the world's most pristine reef and a natural world heritage site. More than 1,500 fish species depended on the reef, as did six of the world's seven species of threatened marine turtles. Today the Great Barrier Reef lies bleached and dead, like the ghostly skeleton of some monstrous, dissected sea creature, its bones picked clean by global warming.

To explain what killed the Great Barrier Reef, I first need to remind your readers of something that schoolchildren used to know back when coral reefs still existed. The colorful coral that we see in old photographs is actually two different creatures. Reefs are made of white calcium carbonate secreted by billions of tiny polyps. The beautiful colors that people used to associate with coral came from a second creature: minute colored plants, or algae, that lived in symbiosis with the polyps. Worldwide, some four thousand fish species depended on those algae.

The sad fact is that when the temperature of seawater rises above 86°F [30°C], coral expels the algae and bleaches to its natural white color. Having nothing left to feed on, the fish and the entire coral ecosystem die. Corals had always bleached during warm-water episodes, but until this century the water would eventually cool and give the corals a chance to recover.

As the twentieth century ended, coral reefs were already in trouble. In an El Niño warming in 1998, the world lost 16 percent of its coral reefs, including parts of the Great Barrier Reef. Then came the summer of 2002, when the surface temperature of the seawater in the southern oceans rose 3.6°F [2°C] above normal and held there for two months, causing extensive bleaching. The summer of 2005 saw the highest ocean temperatures since satellite measurements began; once again, many individual reefs bleached and died. Between 2014 and 2017, just three years, the coral cover in the north region of the reef had dropped by half. Two severe cyclones contributed but did so much damage because the coral was already weakened. These events were before global warming really got going, mind you.

The Australians did what they could to try to protect the reef. They adopted no-fishing zones, cleaned up the water entering the ocean off Queensland, and ended seafloor trawling by the Japanese and other nations. But they could not cool the oceans. By 2050, 95 percent of the Great Barrier Reef had died, taking with it more than a thousand fish species. The beautiful reef that once brought Australia well over $1 billion in tourism annually then brought in nothing.

As for another tourist attraction, Australia's famous beaches, no one would want to come here for them. The beaches have shrunk and disappeared and on many, stinging and sometimes deadly jellyfish now clog the nearshore waters and their bodies litter the sand. The jellyfish are the cockroaches of the sea—the ultimate survivor. If we had wanted to create a jellyfish factory, we could not have done it any better. We fished out their predators—the game fish like sharks, tuna, and swordfish. We polluted the ocean and lowered the nearshore oxygen content. Then we warmed the seas. The result? A jellyfish explosion. A jellyfish sting is not just a matter of temporary inconvenience. The stings can cause painful wounds that do not heal for months. Worse, if the Irukandji jellyfish stings you, you get severe pain in your arms, legs, back, and kidneys. Your skin begins to burn, your head hurts, you become nauseated and vomit, and your heart rate and blood pressure shoot up. Then, in some cases, you die. Risk all that for a day at the beach? No thank you. If you go to an Australian beach today, instead of people you will find the bodies of thousands or tens of thousands of jellyfish. The smell alone is enough to drive people away.

Near the Great Barrier Reef lay another world heritage site: the Wet Tropics of Queensland rain forest. Whereas the reef spread out laterally along the seafloor, the rain forest ranged vertically up the steep slopes of the coastal mountains of northeast Queensland, whose peaks rise sharply from sea level to over 1 mile [1,500 meters] in elevation. A unique plant community had evolved on the peaks by extracting moisture directly from the clouds that covered the summits.

The rain forest once held seven hundred plant species, many of them found nowhere else on Earth. Some had not changed since the dinosaurs. But as temperatures climbed, the cloud layer on which the trees, frogs, snakes, and even microbes in the soil depended, rose higher, then out of reach, and then finally burned away. More than three-fourths of the forest's bird species became extinct. Such creatures as the golden bowerbird, the cassowary, Victoria's riflebird, wompoo pigeon, shining starling, orange-footed scrub fowl, paradise kingfisher, green ringtail possum, the striped possum, tree kangaroo, musky rat-kangaroo, coppery brushtail possum, northern bettong, and the six Gliders: the mahogany, squirrel, greater, feathertail, sugar, and yellow-bellied—all these and many others are gone from the Wet Tropics of Queensland and from our planet for all time.

Dr. Landry, the IUCN is dedicated to the conservation of species, yet this century has already seen the greatest species extinction since the end of the Cretaceous Period 65 million years ago. Pardon me for being so personal, but in the face of such massive losses, how do you keep your balance and your motivation?

As you know, my predecessor found that such a difficult question to answer that she took her own life. The few of us left in conservation work today understand that we are working far beyond triage—that the best we can hope to do is save a tiny sample of the diversity of life that once existed, and the only way we can do even that is by trying to preserve species in zoos. What keeps us going then? I suppose it is the knowledge that if we do not try to save the few species that we can, who will? But why save species, people ask me, isn't it hopeless? That is like asking a religious person why they have faith. Both come from deep inside. You cannot really explain your faith to someone else—instead, it is something you have to act on because you believe.

Review for my readers the overall state of species extinction during this century of global warming.

I'll begin by speaking generally and then give a few examples from among the tens of thousands of twenty-first-century extinctions. I'll start with the birds. Each bird species has a certain habitat—a particular combination of temperature, precipitation, vegetation, insect

life, and the like—in which it thrives. When lowland habitats grow
too warm, a plant community can move uphill to higher slopes that
had been cooler—if such slopes exist—and the birds can follow. But
eventually this strategy falls victim to geometry. The higher a species ascends a mountain, the less the area there is at any one elevation—think of a volcanic cone that rises to an apex. The shrinking
habitat inevitably crowds individuals and species together and that
alone causes extinctions. But as the temperature keeps rising, habitats simply migrate to the top of the mountain and disappear, taking
the dependent species with them. That is what happened not only in
the Queensland rain forest but in mountainous regions and on islands
around the world.

You would think that birds, being able to fly, could easily follow
their habitat as it shifts. If it got too warm in one place, a species could
simply move its range to a cooler place. The problem was that 80 percent of all birds are sedentary—they fly poorly or prefer life on the
ground or in the brush to life in the treetops. As temperatures rose
and habitats migrated, these birds had no way of following. Large
numbers of bird species have already gone extinct and many more are
on the brink. Of the many thousands of bird species extant at the turn
of the century, we estimate that half are extinct today. This was a long
time coming and was foreseen. A scientific study published in 2019
found that one-quarter of North America's birds—3 billion breeding
adults—had been killed by human impacts in the preceding fifty years.
The white-throated sparrow, loved by every birder and common to
backyard feeders, lost 93 million individuals. Remember, this was just
on one continent—North America—and much of the loss had occurred before global warming had really gotten started. Did any of the
deniers take note of this avian holocaust and decide there might be
something to global warming? No, these were people prepared to sac-

rifice their grandchildren's future for the sake of their ideology—and what did birds matter, anyway?

I shudder to imagine how few of the world's birds will be left at the end of this century of death. A twentieth-century author wrote of a silent spring. We may be facing a future when the forests, mountain slopes, wetlands, savannas, and other bird habitats fall silent not just for the spring but for every season and for eternity.

Tens of thousands of other animal species large and small have gone extinct as well—no one will ever know how many. The devastating fires in Australia at the end of 2019 were estimated to have killed 1 billion animals, including the koala, the kangaroo, and many other species that exist nowhere else. But did this awful fact penetrate the hard hearts of Australia's deniers in government and the media? No. They just tried to find someone else to blame for the fires.

When global warming began to accelerate at the beginning of the twenty-first century, the polar bear became the iconic species threatened. Now it is gone, the last one seen in the wild in 2031. Twelve penguin species have gone extinct: the Galapagos penguin, emperor penguin, northern and southern rockhopper penguins, Fiordland crested penguin, Snares crested penguin, erect-crested penguin, macaroni penguin, royal penguin, white-flippered penguin, yellow-eyed penguin, African penguin, and Humboldt penguin. Readers may find it tiresome for me to recite lists of species names, but as I speak their names, I speak for them, to prevent them from becoming lost to human memory. Like Maya Lin, who designed the old Vietnam Veterans Memorial in Washington, D.C., with the name of each fallen soldier carved into stone, I want to carve the names of these fallen species into the stone of history.

We tend to focus on the loss of larger, charismatic species, like the mountain gorilla and the orangutan, both extinct in the wild, though both were as much the victim of desperate poaching and government neglect as global warming.

At the opposite end of the size scale, the little pika, a small mammal that lived in high mountain rock piles and that was the favorite of hikers in your Rocky Mountains, is no more. Pika habitats moved upslope and disappeared, or moved north, but the little animal could not follow. In its entire lifetime, a pika might have moved no more than a kilometer and to survive global warming, it would have had to travel much farther than that, putting survival out of reach. I speak for the pika and I mourn its loss.

The magnificent Bengal tiger was last seen in the Sundarbans mangrove swamp in southern Bangladesh in 2038. But who records the loss of less well-known Sundarbans species like the estuarine crocodile, river terrapin, the Ganges River dolphin, the dog-faced water snake, and the mouse gecko? For every species that we know has gone extinct, logic demands that countless others we had yet to discover have gone extinct too.

The greatest percentage of extinctions may have occurred out of sight, in the oceans. The more carbon dioxide seawater absorbs, the more acidic it becomes, dissolving the calcium carbonate shells of marine organisms, including coral reefs. This process has caused the extinction of many species of plankton, starfish, urchins, oysters, coral polyps, as well as the larger species like squid that feed on them. No one has any idea how many species the acidic ocean has lost, but the number is bound to be astronomical.

Many species of the larger fish that humans once ate have also gone extinct. As competition for food became fiercer, nations began to disregard the treaties that had kept them from completely fishing out a species. As a sample, let me recite the number of extinct whale and cetacean species that have gone extinct: northern right, southern right, bowhead, blue, fin, sei, humpback, and sperm whales. Among the other cetaceans the vaquita, baiji, Indus susu, Ganges susu, boto, franciscana, tucuxi, Hector's dolphin, Indo-Pacific humpbacked dolphin, and Atlantic humpbacked dolphin.

I could go on listing individual species that we know have gone extinct, but it would take not just the rest of your book but an encyclopedia. What I will say instead is that the planet has lost not only individual species, not only ecosystems, but on some continents whole clusters of ecosystems. For this decimation, only one word will do: biocide.

Early in the century, scientists tried to forecast how many species might be lost. They looked at species already endangered and tried to imagine how global warming might affect them. They did not foresee that nearly the entire Amazon would burn, that the Australian outback grasslands and the Sahel would revert to desert, that 620 miles [1,000 km] of the Murray–Darling system would simply dry up, that the Colorado River Delta would dry up, that vast tracts of forests would burn. They did not imagine that a lack of water would lead to war, much less atomic war, which destroyed all life in sections of the Punjab, including innumerable species.

The worst-case projection early in the century was that global warming would cost one-third of all species. Of course, no one knew then how many species the Earth actually had. Scientists had named only about 2 million species; estimates of the total varied from 5 to 30 million. The best estimate of the IUCN today is that about two-thirds of species extant in the year 2000 are now extinct. If we take the midpoint of the 5 to 30 million range, 17.5 million, as the roughest of estimates, two-thirds corresponds to about 12 million species—not individuals, I am not talking about that—but species. The number of individuals lost is as the stars in the heavens.

The IUCN used to maintain a Red List of particularly threatened species but gave that up as pointless. As of 2005, the Red List contained 12,200 species and another 6,300 that were coendangered: that is, whose survival depended on another endangered species also surviving. We estimate that 95 percent of the Red List and codependent species have gone extinct.

But Dr. Landry, a reader might well ask, where is your sense of proportion? Hundreds of millions of human beings have died as well and the world teems with climate refugees, millions of whom are bound to die prematurely. Does the loss of a single species not pale in comparison to the greatest loss of life in human history? Let me challenge you to defend one species chosen at random: What does the extinction of the green ringtail possum from the Wet Tropics of Queensland matter to us humans? What good was it to us?

That is a question that conservationists ask themselves constantly. It is our ultimate question and one that each of us has to answer for himself or herself. What I am about to say is my own, deeply personal answer. Of course, we should preserve species and ecosystems because they have practical benefits and we do not know in advance what those benefits may be. Vital medicines, vaccines, and the like have come from rare species. One estimate at the turn of the century was that tropical rain forests supplied 25 percent of our medicines. But scientists had been able to test only 1 percent of species. Who knows what important medicines no one had yet discovered? And now no one ever will, because the species that could have provided them have gone extinct.

But I understand that as far as we know and ever will know, the little possum that you named provided no such benefits. So, your question is a fair one: What good was the green ringtail possum? In my

202 JAMES LAWRENCE POWELL

opinion there are two answers, and either or both will do. A religious person believes God created all life on Earth, including the possum. In the words of an old hymn, then God's "eye is on the sparrow": He watches over even the lowest of His creatures and it ought to be the sacred obligation of each devout person to do the same. By honoring His creatures, we honor Him. What right do we have to destroy God's creations and replace His plan with our own? Perhaps His judgment will rest on how well we have served as stewards of the Earth and all His creatures. If so, humanity is doomed to eternal hellfire, for we have failed abysmally. Maybe hell is already with us. Maybe this, and what lies ahead for our planet, is hell, God's terrible retribution for our failure.

Now, it is true that God's plan must have included extinction, for the vast majority of species that ever existed have gone extinct naturally. Mysterious are His ways. But the fact of natural extinction does not justify the human race taking over God's timetable and His prerogatives. One can imagine the God of the Old Testament booming from the heavens: "Who do you think you are?"

Few scientists, even religious ones, believe in such a literal interpretation of the Bible, as I do not. Instead we accept that the possum and every other creature on Earth is the product of millions of years of evolution. Some even believe, as I do, that given the number of random events that had to take place to produce advanced life-forms like the possum and *Homo sapiens*, it is unlikely that mammals, say, exist anywhere else in the universe. Those who hold this view see life on Earth as just as miraculous and magnificent as those who believe it is God's creation. We do not wish to be responsible for carelessly snuffing out species four billion years in the making.

Personally, I believe that life must be worth preserving—all life, including the green ringtail possum. For me, not to believe that is to regard life itself as meaningless and then I might as well not believe in anything, as indeed many today no longer do. Whatever your belief system, if life matters, you cannot single out one species and say that particular one does not matter. They all matter. If the green ringtail possum does not matter, then life does not matter, you and I do not matter, and Earth, the only planet to bear intelligent life, does not matter. I cannot accept *that* philosophy and go on living.

Dr. Landry, as we chatted before the interview, you told me of one subject that you wanted to be able to talk about, one we might call a different kind of animal extinction. Let me give you that chance now.

Thank you for remembering. This will seem to be a change of subject and maybe it is, but I still need to get it off my chest. When I think of the sad fate of endangered species, I am reminded of another group of animals for whom I have a special fondness and which have also become victims of global warming. I speak of our pets. This is not what you asked me to talk about, so you can decide whether to include it. As a pet lover, a person who once cohabited with cats, dogs, and horses, this subject is as painful for me to discuss as any of the many painful topics that are going to appear in your book. It breaks my heart to talk about it, but it must be said.

Let's use as a case study the fate of pets in New Orleans during one of the first climate-related disasters: Hurricane Katrina in 2005. A poll taken the next year found that nearly half the people who chose not to evacuate New Orleans stayed because they could not bear to abandon their pets. Think of that. Nothing speaks so loudly of the bond we humans have formed with animals. Even so, the Louisiana SPCA estimated that more than 100,000 pets were left behind and as many as 70,000 died throughout the Gulf Coast. This was a macabre portent of what was to come.

By now, the Earth has experienced innumerable climate disasters on the scale of Katrina, each taking its toll on human life and property, but especially on pets. Just as after the Fall of Berlin near the end of World War II, in most large cities today neither a dog nor a cat is to be seen—only the rats have survived. Having a pet is now a thing of the past and whatever dogs and cats are left have turned feral and are doomed.

I confess to holding a view that may seem odd for such an old sobersides, as friends have called me. It stems in part from the historical record of the domestication of the dog, something as a scientist I know about. The oldest known evidence dates to 14,300 years ago, and shows humans buried beside a dog. The only human remains found at the famous La Brea Tar Pits in Los Angeles dated to about ten thousand years ago and were of a woman buried with a dog, suggesting a ceremonial burial. To have a pet is one thing, to want to take it with you into the Great Beyond is quite another and speaks of a bond between humans and animals that transcends life itself, that is eternal.

In my view, you see, our earliest ancestors made an implicit covenant with the first wolves that became tame enough to be domesticated. Think of it as a mutual-benefit pact: "If you will come in from the cold and befriend our kind, we will do our best to shelter, feed, and protect your kind. We are in it together." We said the same to the horse. And just think of what the dog and the horse have done for us throughout history. Humanity has willfully broken these age-old covenants and if there is a God, I doubt he will forgive us—and he ought not.

PART 9
A WAY OUT

To end this book, I interview Dr. Robert Stapledon and his wife, Dr. Rosetta Stapledon, professors at the University of Toronto until their retirements in the late 2060s. His academic specialty was energy production, hers the history of the failed attempts of governments to limit the global temperature rise to 3.6°F [2°C] through the United Nations, the Paris Agreement on Climate Change, the short-lived Green New Deal, and so on.

Robert and Rosetta, as you have asked me to address you, as you know you will have the last word in this oral history of the Great Warming. One question has loomed over each interview I've conducted, one that is always on the lips of our children and grandchildren. It goes something like this: Grandpa (in my case), people knew that global warming was going to be bad, why didn't they stop it?

My question to you is whether it could have been stopped. When was the last time nations could have at least tried to limit global warming? Was there a point of no return and when was it passed? Robert, let me ask you to begin there.

Robert: As I am sure you have found with many of your subjects, this interview gives us a chance to get something important off our chests, in our case, to put a coda to our scholarly work and careers. If we sound well-rehearsed, it is because we have spent many family dinners and faculty-room conversations on the great questions you raise.

One of the world's attempts to answer these questions was the Paris Agreement on Climate Change, which Rosetta will say more about. Its target had been to limit global warming to 2.7°F [1.5°C] above preindustrial temperatures. But already by the late 2010s, scientists had concluded that no matter what was done, the temperature rise was going to cross that level in 2040 or thereabouts. As we know, they were right. That much heat was already baked in, you might say, and the opportunity to meet that target had passed. The next target was a 3.6°F [2°C] rise, which was reachable if—full caps IF—emissions had peaked and begun to fall by 2020. The job had to begin then, or each subsequent year of delay would make that target harder to reach, and in a decade or so, impossible. So, when scholars like me look back, we judge 2020 to have been the point of no return.

Rosetta: The problem was that like each of the old international climate compacts, starting with the one that came out of the Rio Summit in 1992, the Paris Agreement didn't require its signatories to do anything in particular. Nations didn't have to set specific reduced emissions targets, only targets that went beyond the previous ones, and if a nation failed to meet its target, there was no penalty. In other words, like all the international compacts, the Paris Agreement was completely voluntary.

It had opened to signatories in 2015 and it went into effect in 2020. President Trump had withdrawn the U.S. from the agreement, but because of the built-in delay, the withdrawal didn't occur until 2020. But even before then, danger signals had already begun to appear.

A 2017 report showed that not a single major country was on track to meet its Paris pledges. In 2018, U.S. carbon emissions rose by more than 3 percent, even though a number of coal plants had been closed. The poor progress on the agreement in the U.S. and other countries showed just how deeply fossil fuels were embedded into the economies of the industrialized nations and how hard it would be to dislodge them. When economies improved, CO_2 emissions went up, and vice versa, a deadly embrace that needed to be severed, something that the nations of the world did not have the will to do.

In 2023, the Paris signatories conducted a scheduled "stocktake" on progress. A number of small nations had succeeded in meeting their targets, but the U.S., China, India, and Japan all lagged, and their collective gap outweighed all the cuts other nations had made.

The real trouble was that the Paris Agreement only went to 2030. The assumption was that after nations had voluntarily met the first set of targets, their success would encourage them to agree to cut emissions further after 2030. Today we know that those initial pledges were not met and that one of humanity's last chances to contain global warming was missed.

There was another problem that people often didn't consider in those days. As an example, I'll use India, whose population in 2020 had reached 1.4 billion. Its people, of course, wanted to have the same advantages as developed countries, which had used fossil-fuel consumption to lift their people out of poverty and provide them with electricity, refrigeration, air-conditioning, cars, hospitals, housing, and so on. Didn't the people of India have the same moral right to those benefits as Americans or Australians? Should Indians have given up those benefits, sacrificing for the countries that had created the problem of global warming in the first place?

Regardless of where a person came down on these questions, it was the leaders of India who would decide and they did, saying in 2017: "Around three-quarters of India's power comes from coal-powered plants and this scenario will not change significantly over the coming decades. Thus, it is important that India increases its domestic coal production." Short of war, how could any nation or group of nations have stopped India from building those coal plants? The only way would have been to show the Indians there was a better way than coal to generate electricity.

Robert: As of 2020, although other ways of generating electricity—like wave action or tides, hydrogen as a fuel, and so on—were on the drawing board, the proven sources were the three fossil fuels—coal, oil, and natural gas—and those that could be considered renewable: hydropower, wind, solar, biomass, nuclear, and geothermal. It was from the latter list that salvation would have to come.

Scientists had shown that if emissions could be cut in half in each decade starting with the twenties, and if better agricultural and forestry practices could have captured more CO_2 from the air, fossil-fuel emissions could have netted out to zero in 2050: problem solved, humanity saved. Thus, the immediate question was which of the non-fossil-fuel technologies, singly or in combination, was ready to go and could be ramped up quickly enough to halve CO_2 emissions starting in the twenties.

Before I answer that, I need to say a word about natural gas, which in the 2010s had come to be used primarily as a way to avoid coal. Natural gas was not a long-term solution, because it is a fossil fuel too. It emits about half as much CO_2 as coal, so swapping natural gas for coal only delays the global temperature rise. It was as if a smoker had cut to one pack a day instead of two—the smoker was still likely to die from lung cancer, only it would take longer.

Hydropower is CO_2-free but has its disadvantages: It destroys wild rivers and their ecosystems, displaces indigenous natives, and is enormously expensive. And in the long run, reservoirs fill with sediment and stop generating power, and are thus at best a temporary fix. Plus, by this century most of the good sites had already been dammed. Existing hydro dams could be part of the effort to reach zero fossil-fuel emissions, but only a part. And in the American Southwest, for example, global warming had reduced the flow of the Colorado River so much that Glen Canyon Dam stopped generating power in 2035. Starting in the 2030s, Hoover Dam often fell below its power pool, leaving people in Las Vegas and Phoenix with not enough water or electricity. So, hydropower was not the panacea it was once seen as.

Geothermal energy worked in countries like Iceland that had active volcanism, but most countries did not. Biomass burning had a place but could not be scaled up enough and as quickly as needed. That left three natural energy sources that were inexhaustible or virtually so: wind, solar, and nuclear.

Rosetta: My maiden name, Malmquist, is a clue to the story. I am of Swedish descent and Sweden had shown how to eliminate fossil-fuel emissions and even allow countries like India to have the electrical power they needed and deserved. In my files I have an expert report written sixty-eight years ago titled: "How to decarbonize? Look to Sweden."

Back in the 1960s and '70s, my grandfather Ingmar Malmquist was an engineer with Vattenfall, the Swedish utility company. At many family gatherings, we heard his stories of how Sweden had led the way, but how few had followed. Back in his day, Sweden got quite a lot of its electricity from hydro dams in the mountains of the north. That was an advantage many mountainous countries enjoyed, especially ones whose peaks held glaciers to serve as frozen water reservoirs. Concern about man-made global warming was not yet on the horizon, not even for most scientists. In the 1960s, Vattenfall planned to dam more rivers to generate the additional power Sweden would need in the coming years, but the sixties were also a time of rising environmental awareness everywhere. Swedish conservationists had begun to point out the serious disadvantages of hydro dams. Their protests led

Vattenfall to agree to give up its plans for new dams and conservationists agreed not to oppose its other energy projects.

But, if not hydropower, what could provide the additional electricity Sweden would need? The people of my grandfather's day wanted to reduce Sweden's dependence on imported oil. This was around the time of the global oil crisis of 1973, remember. Sweden could have expanded coal mining, but instead it made a different choice, one that had the unsought benefit of reducing overall CO_2 emissions.

From 1960 to the mid-1970s, Swedish CO_2 emissions per person rose at the same rate as its GDP, again showing how the two were linked. But by 1990 GDP per person had doubled, yet CO_2 emissions and CO_2 as a percent of total energy production had both been cut roughly in half. Sweden had severed the Gordian knot that bound economic progress and fossil-fuel consumption. It had done in fifteen years what the world needed to do in the decade of the 2020s and beyond. And Sweden had done so without facing an urgent threat from man-made global warming.

But Rosetta, what did Sweden have to give up to achieve those results?

Nothing. In 1975, Sweden's GDP per capita was about the same as the U.S. For the next forty years, the two grew at the same rate. Since GDP per capita is a good proxy for quality of life, in those forty years, Sweden achieved the same improvement in living standards as the U.S. but did so while cutting CO_2 emissions drastically. They did so using nuclear reactors.

Nuclear energy was carbon-free like hydropower, cheaper than oil, much less detrimental to health than coal, so concentrated that it produces little waste, and a proven and widespread technology. True, anything nuclear was always controversial, but in the 1970s, it had not yet become anathema to environmentalists.

Starting in the 1970s, Sweden built twelve commercial nuclear reactors on four sites. By the 1980s, the cost of electricity in Sweden had fallen to one of the lowest in the world. The cost of running the nuclear plants was lower than any energy source other than existing hydropower. Sweden retired its fossil-fuel plants and over time doubled its electricity consumption, including a five-fold increase in the use of nuclear-generated electricity for heating.

But Sweden is a small country. Could the nuclear solution also work for larger nations?

Yes, as we know from France which also went heavily into nuclear power in the 1970s, building fifty-six new reactors in fifteen years, greatly lowering its emissions and the cost of electricity. Another example is Ontario, where we live. Between 1976 and 1993, Ontario built sixteen new reactors, allowing nuclear energy to supply 60 percent of the province's power and existing hydropower most of the rest. Fossil fuels were on the way out.

These experiments showed that a worldwide ramp-up of nuclear power at the same rate as those countries had done could replace fossil fuels within about twenty-five years.

What about the rest of the world? Had other countries also embraced nuclear power?

By the late 2010s, thirty-one countries were operating 449 power-generating reactors and producing about 10 percent of the world's electricity. Of the total number, ninety-nine of those reactors were in the U.S., where they generated 20 percent of electricity. Thus, even though for many environmental organizations nuclear power was off the table, by the 2010s its use was widespread, successful, and growing. What was needed was more of it.

Ramping up nuclear power on the model of Sweden and France could only have been done quickly enough in countries that already had experience with nuclear regulations and licensing. Almost all the large carbon emitters met those requirements.

Robert and Rosetta, if I could sum up before we take a break, you are saying that several countries, including Canada, France, and Sweden, had shown that an expansion of nuclear power production could have cut fossil-fuel emissions enough between 2020 and 2050 to keep the global temperature rise under 3.6°F [2°C] and to eliminate fossil-fuel use. More than two dozen countries, including the U.S., China, Russia, and India, had the necessary experience and controls. And yet it was not done. I have to tell you that this is a very hard thing to hear. Surely, to avoid what in hindsight appears to have been the only way out, people in the tens and twenties must have had a very good reason for not turning to nuclear power. When we return, I will ask you to explain that reason.

Robert and Rosetta, to restate the question with which we ended yesterday: If following the example of Sweden in particular, nuclear power production could have been ramped up far enough and fast enough to have essentially eliminated fossil-fuel consumption by 2050, why wasn't it done?

Robert: The answer is simple: because people were afraid of all things nuclear. This attitude persisted even though, as we discussed last time, the actual practice in more than two dozen countries had shown that the reasons behind the prejudice were groundless. This fear, combined with continued denial of man-made global warming, delayed the eventual ramp-up and caused it to begin too late.

Let's take the objections to nuclear power one by one. Remember, I am talking here about what people knew, or should have known, as of about 2020, by which time nuclear reactors had been in use for sixty years. We have an extensive library of old reports and articles from that period that I will refer to as necessary, to show that what I am saying is not just coming from an old man's faulty memory.

By far the most important objection was the perception—not the fact, as I will show, the perception—that nuclear power is inherently unsafe. Where did that attitude come from? Since the use of atomic bombs on Hiroshima and Nagasaki in 1945 and the escalating nuclear arms race with the Soviet Union during the Cold War, people around the world had come to fear not just the direct blast effects of nuclear weapons, but the long-lived and dangerous radiation that they release. Schoolchildren practiced "duck and cover," as if their school desk would have provided protection in case of nuclear war. For those generations, the fear of nuclear radiation was ingrained. Every decade or so, a nuclear accident would seem to validate those fears.

One such accident was the 1979 partial meltdown of a reactor at Three Mile Island on the Susquehanna River in Pennsylvania, caused by both mechanical and human failures. The accident came twelve days after the premiere of a nuclear disaster movie called *The China Syndrome*, which reinforced people's fears. But, in fact, the containment structure at TMI worked as designed and the accident had no immediate health effects. There was a lot of worry about long-term effects from the radiation released, but scientists later found little evidence of them. The damage to perception, however, had been done.

Next came the 1986 accident at Chernobyl in Ukraine when it was part of the old Soviet Union. The Soviets designed their reactors to make plutonium for weapons while also producing power. This required them to use graphite to control the nuclear reactions and water to keep the fuel from overheating, an unsafe combination that other nations had avoided and that invited operator error. The reactor, unlike Three Mile Island, had no containment vessel and would have been illegal in the U.S. During a test with the safety systems turned off, the poor design and operator mistakes caused the release of a large amount of radiation. As a weapons plant, Chernobyl was supposed to be secret so Soviet officials lied about the accident and did not issue radiation-absorbing iodine pills to protect local residents. A Belarussian physicist working in Minsk, almost 300 miles [482 km] from Chernobyl, only learned of the accident when he found that the radiation detectors outside his lab were registering higher levels than those inside. Several dozen of the first responders at Chernobyl died fighting the resulting fires and later from exposure to radiation. Estimating the future number of deaths from radiation exposure at Chernobyl caused a great controversy, but in 2005 a team of more than one hundred scientists estimated the death toll at four thousand. But in the late 2010s, there were books and films about Chernobyl that reinforced the fear of everything nuclear. Yet Chernobyl was not an inevitability, but the product of a defective reactor design and a defective political system.

Then in 2011 came a massive earthquake and resulting 50-foot [15-meter] tsunami in Japan, near Fukushima and its nuclear power plants. The Japanese Nuclear and Industrial Safety Agency had told Tokyo Electric Power, the operating company, to ensure that the reactors could survive a predictable tsunami. A 46-foot [14-meter] seawall protected the three reactors at the Onagawa site, allowing them to shut down normally after the earthquake with no injuries or loss of life. The Daiichi plant was farther away from the epicenter and behind a seawall only 20 feet [6 meters] tall. All the backup generators were placed behind this wall, which the tsunami overtopped, causing the generators to fail. Hydrogen gas exploded and broke the containment vessel, releasing radiation into the surrounding area and the nearby ocean. Japanese officials evacuated more than 150,000 residents, a process that cost the lives of about fifty people.

A study by the old World Health Organization estimated how many people were at long-term risk of contracting cancer from the Fukushima radiation. The report used the worst-case "linear no-threshold" model for estimating future radiation effects, which assumed that even the smallest amount of radiation was harmful, including the amounts to which we are normally exposed each day from burning coal or living on granitic soil, for example. It concluded that the impact on public health would be small. Of course, every life is precious, but that ought to have motivated people to choose the energy source that saved the most.

Each of these accidents, and further advances in nuclear engineering, led to safety improvements. For example, after the Chernobyl accident, engineers developed "walk-away safe," third-generation reactors that would shut down and prevent a meltdown automatically for seventy-two hours or longer.

Any way you look at it, coal power was proven to be vastly more dangerous than nuclear. For instance, during the experience with nuclear power between the 1960s and 2020, tens of millions had died from burning coal—mainly from cancer-causing particulates—and nuclear power had cost at most several thousand lives. Looking at the rate of death per unit of power, coal had caused about thirty deaths per terawatt-hour, while nuclear energy had caused about 0.1.

People who wanted to ban the use of nuclear power were in effect choosing a known and deadly killer, coal, over a technology that had been proven to be much safer and, instead of destroying the world, might save it. Now factor into the decision the number who have died and will die as a result of global warming. To save the thousands of lives that might have been lost to nuclear power accidents, and the actual number might have turned out to be much lower, hundreds of millions, perhaps a billion, lives were lost to global warming. And it is not over.

Beyond the safety issue, what were some of the other concerns about nuclear power?

Robert: One that hearkened back to the Cold War decades was that widespread use of nuclear power would lead to a proliferation of nuclear weapons. While Russia, the U.S., and several other nations already collectively had thousands of nuclear warheads, the concern was that nations like Iran could quickly convert nuclear power reactors to build nuclear weapons. These were not idle concerns, but by the late 2010s the world had sixty years of experience showing that nuclear energy programs had not led to weapons.

One of the reasons was the success of the International Atomic Energy Agency (IAEA), a watchdog established by the UN in 1957 to promote peaceful uses of nuclear energy and deter its use for war. One success story occurred when the IAEA descended on Saddam Hussein's Iraq but could find no evidence that he was developing nuclear weapons: because he was not. Of course, that scientific conclusion conflicted with political ideology and so it was ignored, and America invaded Iraq at a cost of nearly two trillion dollars. Think what else could have been done with that money.

Let's go back to 1967, by which time five nations had detonated a nuclear weapon: the United States, the Soviet Union, the United Kingdom, France, and China. They were the signatories of the original Treaty on the Non-Proliferation of Nuclear Weapons, as well as the permanent members of the UN Security Council. Later, three countries that were not part of the treaty also tested a nuclear weapon: India, North Korea, and Pakistan. Israel was believed to have nuclear weapons, bringing the total to nine. But none of those programs had emerged from the use of nuclear power reactors. The Soviets tried it and got the Chernobyl accident instead.

Another concern was that nuclear power was thought to be uneconomical and too slow to develop compared to other energy sources. One reason that building nuclear power plants had been so expensive and time-consuming was that in the U.S. and some European countries, resistance by anti-nuclear groups and the resulting litigation and delay caused the projects to exceed their budgets and timetables. But Sweden's costs were competitive with other energy sources and South Korea and others had begun to build cheaper reactors. Sweden decided to build its reactors before the accidents I have reviewed, and thus before a substantial protest movement had developed. To convert to nuclear power took Sweden only fifteen to twenty years.

A subject that understandably worried people was how to dispose of the radioactive waste from nuclear reactors. The worry was made worse in the U.S. by the much-publicized controversy over the use of Yucca Mountain, Nevada, as a disposal site. *A Bright Future*, the book that Rosetta and I have used as background, pointed out that if all the electricity an average American used in a lifetime back then had come from coal, the resulting solid waste would weigh 136,000 pounds [61,689 kg]. But if the same amount of power had come from nuclear energy, the waste would weigh about 2 pounds [0.9 kg] and as the authors said, "fit in a soda can."

By the twenties nuclear reactors had been around for sixty years and nearly five hundred had been built, yet there had been only a handful of incidents resulting from waste disposal and none had any health effects. A number of countries were developing fourth-generation reactors that would consume their own waste. Yes, waste was something to worry about, something to be monitored carefully, but it was not a reason to forgo nuclear energy.

Rosetta: By the beginning of this century, people had begun to focus more on "renewables," particularly solar and wind energy. These were critically important, but by 2020 not enough had been deployed to give them any chance of producing the amount of carbon-free energy needed to save humanity. Since the sun shines only part of the time and the wind does not always blow, each had the problem of "intermittency," with no good way to store the energy until it was needed.

The Germans had gone heavily into renewables, but used them to replace nuclear, leaving their dependence on fossil fuels unchanged and the world worse off, not better off. The old Green New Deal had urged getting to 100 percent renewables in only one decade, but that was infeasible. Had our predecessors gone the nuclear route, by the time they got rid of fossil fuels in 2050, say, solar and wind technology would have been far advanced and could have begun to replace some of the then-aging nuclear power plants. The storage problem could have been solved. If nations so chose, they could then have weaned themselves off nuclear power and achieved 100 percent renewable energy.

There was also a common belief that nuclear power was so controversial that expanding it was impossible politically. But if anything was politically infeasible, it was action on global warming. If resistance to stopping global warming could have been overcome, a nuclear solution would not only have been feasible, but necessary. This was just a self-fulfilling and dangerous prophecy.

Another way to reduce dependence on fossil fuels was to tax their production. I understand that Sweden did something like that as well.

Rosetta: Yes, it did. Taxing is one way government can disincentivize undesirable practices. Economists and climate scientists had long advocated taxing fossil-fuel production, at the wellhead or mine, not at the pump or meter. Without some such tax, the public and not the companies had to pay for all the present and future costs of using fossil fuels. As someone said, the companies had privatized the profits while outsourcing the costs to the public, a sweet deal for them and a catastrophe for humanity.

In 1991, when the new reactors were producing at their peak and after its carbon emissions had already declined a lot, Sweden took the next step and became one of the first countries to adopt a carbon tax. The initial rate was $25 [23 EUR] per ton of carbon produced. At the same time as the imposition of the tax, Sweden wisely got rid of most other energy taxes, increasing the incentive for companies to move to low-carbon sources but without the government dictating which ones.

Another thing that economists had long agreed about was that however carbon was taxed or priced, it needed to start low and increase over time. That would give households and businesses time to adapt and signal that producing energy from fossil fuels was a losing game. By 2020 Sweden's tax had risen to about $119 [110 EUR] per ton. California had adopted a cap-and-trade method, but it priced carbon at only $15 [13.5 EUR] per ton, clearly too low. Sweden's tax revenues gave it the money to offset the undesired effects of the tax and fund other climate-related measures.

Summing up what you two have told me, starting around 2020 the major emitters could have ramped up nuclear power and ended fossil-fuel consumption by 2050. Yet because of unfounded concerns over nuclear energy, they did not take that action until too late. Review for my readers the sad story of what happened instead.

Rosetta: As you know, a number of books have been written on that question, including one by the two of us. Rather than dictating another one, let's summarize. The 2020s were the critical decade and humanity's last chance to gain control of its future. And the U.S. was the critical country, not only because it was the second-biggest polluter but because it was the nation others had once looked to as a leader.

Signatories to the Paris Agreement built new nuclear reactors and introduced a carbon tax, but they did not start until near the end of the twenties, and whatever emissions cuts they had made were significantly offset by the rise in those of the U.S., China, and India. And don't forget Japan, which chose collective seppuku by building twenty-five new coal-fired plants in the twenties. This was the bitter fruit of overreaction to the preventable Fukushima accident.

The new president from the America First Party took office and brought the U.S. back into the Paris Agreement, but it was only symbolic. Other nations began to conclude that the efforts to contain global warming were likely to fail, so when the agreement expired in 2030, many shifted their spending from reducing emissions to trying to mitigate the effects of global warming, such as by building high seawalls and evacuating people from coastal zones. Even then, people just could not seem to get their head around the fact that if the ice caps melted, there would be no seawall high enough.

One curious, or maybe tragic, thing that some scholars have noted is that for the last two decades, global CO_2 emissions from fossil fuels have fallen and at some point in the next century will reach zero. There has been a weird kind of feedback at work in which emitting CO_2 eventually destroys the infrastructure necessary to emit more CO_2. But the enormous amount put into the atmosphere in the twenty-first century will still be up there, absorbing heat rays and raising temperature, for millennia.

I know that Robert has one last point, one that we agree on, so I will turn to him to finish our interview.

Robert: There was one thing that might have been expected in the twenties that did not happen and that could have forced governments to act quickly to reduce emissions. I have in mind the kinds of mass protests and strikes that had marked previous struggles against governments that had failed to listen. You could start with the American Revolution and go on to women's suffrage, China's May Fourth Movement, civil rights, the fight against apartheid, protests against the war in Vietnam, France's May 68, Solidarity, the Icelandic women's strike in 1975, the Berlin Wall coming down, the Arab Spring, the Catalan independence uprising, the West Virginia teachers' strike, and so on. People were willing to protest and strike for a host of reasons and they often won. Why then didn't those whose grandchildren's future was at stake, alongside possibly that of civilization itself, not rise up and demand government action to reduce CO_2 emissions, and, if the government refused, take to the streets and put their lives on the line to shut it down? Were they sheep or human beings?

You have reached the end, and I thank you for reading. Permit me to pass along a few final thoughts of my own.

At several points the question has arisen of why our predecessors, who could not reasonably have denied that global warming is real, caused by humans, and dangerous, did not stop it.

When I first became interested in the effect global warming would have on humanity, back when the Internet was still working, I reviewed videos of the State of the Union messages of U.S. presidents from 2000 through 2028. I also reviewed a sample of each of the presidential debates during that period. In all those millions of spoken words, global warming almost never came up. I don't blame the politicians entirely, for they could not get too far ahead of the public and hope to win an election. And what was public opinion? In 2007, a U.S. poll showed that "dealing with global warming" ranked second to last of sixteen concerns. In 2019, it remained second to last.

Scientists, the media, and writers failed to get across to the public just how bad global warming was going to be, and that on our human timescale it would effectively last for eternity. The question that understandably tantalizes me is whether, if I could step into a time machine and go back to the early 2020s to put this book in people's hands, it would have made any difference. If not, then the great science fiction writer Walter Miller had it right in *A Canticle for Leibowitz*: Something is wrong with us. We have the intellectual ability to invent the means of our own destruction, but not the reasoning ability to stop ourselves from using it.

James Lawrence Powell graduated from Berea College with a degree in geology. He earned a PhD in geochemistry from the Massachusetts Institute of Technology and has several honorary degrees, including Doctor of Science degrees from Berea College and Oberlin College. He taught geology at Oberlin College for over twenty years and served as acting president of Oberlin, president of Franklin & Marshall College, president of Reed College, president of the Franklin Institute Science Museum in Philadelphia, and president and director of the Los Angeles County Museum of Natural History. President Reagan, and later President George H. W. Bush, appointed him to the National Science Board, where he served for twelve years. Asteroid 1987 SH7 is named for him. In 2015, he was elected a Fellow of the Committee for Skeptical Inquiry (CSI).